THE
STRESS
MYTH

Richard E. Ecker

Why the Pressures of Life
Don't Have to
Get You Down

InterVarsity Press
DOWNERS GROVE, ILLINOIS 60515

InterVarsity Press is the book-publishing division of Inter-Varsity Christian Fellowship, a student movement active on campus at hundreds of universities, colleges and schools of nursing. For information about local and regional activities, write IVCF, 233 Langdon St., Madison, WI 53703.

Distributed in Canada through InterVarsity Press, 860 Denison St., Unit 3, Markham, Ontario L3R 4H1, Canada.

Scripture quotations are from the Revised Standard Version of the Bible, copyrighted 1946, 1952, © 1971, 1973.

Cover illustration: Roberta Polfus

ISBN 0-87784-330-9

Printed in the United States of America

Library of Congress Cataloging in Publication Data
Ecker, Richard E., 1930-
    The stress myth.

    Bibliography: p.
        1. Stress (Psychology)   2. Stress (Psychology)—
Prevention.   I. Title.
BF575.S75E28   1985   158'.1   85-220
ISBN 0-87784-330-9

15	14	13	12	11	10	9	8	7	6	5	4	3	2	1
95	94	93	92	91	90	89	88	87	86	85				

And which of you by
being anxious can add one cubit
to his span of life?
Matthew 6:27

1 The Stress Myth

SHUT IT DOWN."

As the emergency room fell silent, Dr. Johnson pulled off his gloves, paused for a moment to look in frustration at the lifeless form on the table beside him and then walked slowly out to the waiting room to inform Rita Chapman that her husband had not survived his heart attack. It was early Monday afternoon. John Chapman had just fallen victim to what in medical circles is called "sudden cardiac death," the most common cause of death in the United States today.

Every week, over eight thousand Americans die suddenly of heart attacks. This in itself is a sobering statistic. But it becomes even more alarming when we consider that far more of these deaths occur on Monday than on any other day (*American Medical News*, May 15, 1981). Why Monday? Because it is the first workday of the week—the day when American workers abandon the relaxing pace of a weekend at home and return to the pressures of life on the job. The unfortunate souls who bow out every Monday as they gear up for the workweek ahead are listed in health statistics as victims of cardiac failure, but the reason for these heart attacks is stress.

The thousands of people who succumb to fatal Monday attacks are but a handful compared to the hordes of Americans who daily suffer discomfort, inconvenience, disability or death as the result of stress. This year, almost a hundred million prescriptions for tranquilizing drugs will be consumed by the American people. Stress-formula vitamins are now among the most popular vitamin preparations in our country, even though they have absolutely no value either for preventing stress or for overcoming any of its effects on the body. Suicide is on the rise, particularly among teen-agers and young adults. Stress has become the most common cause of job dissatisfaction, of reduced productivity in the workplace, and of family conflict and divorce.

Unquestionably, stress is the most significant negative health influence at work in American society today, and the problem grows more serious every day. Why is our society so devastated by stress? Why do we seem unable to stem its tide of physical and social degeneration? We like to believe that stress is inevitable—that life is so much more complex these days, that we're being dragged along by a runaway world which offers us less and less we can depend on. But that belief is nothing but a myth, a myth that is at the core of the stress problem. We're not victims of a life full of uncertainty. We're victims of the myth that uncertainty inevitably leads us into unwanted stress.

Is Stress Inevitable?
This myth, which I call the *stress myth*, has done more to perpetuate unwanted stress in our society than any other single factor. Ironically, the main proponents of the myth are the very ones who claim to be teaching people how to deal with stress. These followers

of the traditional school of stress education teach that we must accept unwanted stress as a fact of life and learn how to live with it. Their approach, which is called *intervention,* is intended to help reduce the damaging effects of unwanted stress after it occurs. Thus they emphasize such techniques as biofeedback, meditation, hypnosis and relaxation. Unfortunately, the cemetery is full of people like John Chapman who are already dead by the time the need for stress intervention becomes apparent. Relaxation techniques, after all, do not help reduce the tensions of rigor mortis.

To free ourselves from unwanted stress, we first must free ourselves from the stress myth—the idea that unwanted stress is inevitable. To do this means learning to employ a constructive alternative to stress intervention. This alternative, called stress *prevention,* eliminates the need for intervention by keeping unwanted stress from ever occurring.

Dr. Denis Burkitt, a noted British physician and authority on the role of lifestyle in human health, uses the following illustration to dramatize the distinction between intervention and prevention. Picture a high cliff atop which people are busily working and playing. There is no guard rail at the rim of the cliff, so frequently a careless individual falls over the edge. Because these accidents are common, a clinic has been set up at the base of the cliff to attend to minor injuries and to transport the seriously wounded to nearby hospitals. The role of the medical team working in the clinic is *intervention:* they accept the injuries as inevitable and plan their strategies on that basis. Simply installing a guard rail at the edge of the cliff would be *prevention.* This strategy anticipates the problem and works to keep it from occurring. (Burkitt gives this illustration in *Eat Right to Stay Healthy and Enjoy Life More* [New York: Arco Publishing Co., 1979], p. 113.)

Prevention frees us from unwanted stress to whatever extent we are willing to work to achieve it. In opting for stress prevention rather than intervention, I am not saying that all intervention is wrong. Some behavior therapists, for example, consider relaxation techniques essential for making their patients receptive to therapy. I do not dispute this practice any more than I would dispute the administration of antibiotics to a patient who has an infection. Yet just as I believe that immunization, hygiene and other preventive measures are the preferred way to avoid infectious disease, so I believe that stress prevention is the preferred way to avoid unwanted stress.

It would be irresponsible to neglect immunization against diphtheria merely because we now have effective antibiotics to treat the disease. I would never advise people to ignore the vaccination and wait until they come down with diphtheria to have it treated. Similarly, I consider it irresponsible to neglect stress prevention just because it is sometimes possible to dissipate existing stress through intervention techniques. The ideal is not to learn to live with unwanted stress, but to learn to keep from having it in the first place.

The problem with stress intervention is not its techniques, but the fact that these techniques have become the primary focus among practitioners who aim to help people deal with stress. Stress intervention accepts unwanted stress as a fact of life and concentrates on teaching people how to live with it. If the same approach were used to control infectious disease—if immunization (prevention) were abandoned in favor of antibiotic therapy (intervention)—offending organisms would prosper in a culture of highly susceptible hosts. The only hope for relief would be in immediate intervention. Very soon, all the antibiotics in the world would be unable to stem the plagues resulting from the uncontrolled proliferation of destructive agents.

There is a significant parallel between this frightening consequence of neglected disease prevention and what can be expected if we neglect stress prevention. The stress myth, suggesting that unwanted stress is unavoidable and can be dealt with only after it exists, promotes the continued existence of debilitating stress. As long as we believe that the only way to deal with stress is to wait for it to appear and then to minimize its destructive effects, we will never develop the skills needed to prevent it. The result will be more unwanted stress and a continually greater need for intervention. This, of course, is good for the business of the interventionists, but bad for society's emotional health.

Thus I am compelled to charge interventionist practitioners with contributing to the growing problem of unwanted stress in modern society. If we do not change this emphasis, the problem will continue to increase and its consequences will grow ever more severe. This is not to suggest that those who are immediately facing severely stress-provoking situations should avoid seeking comfort and counsel from people who are skilled in administering such therapy. It merely points out that, in the long run, there is a better way. My calling is to help people understand and apply that better way.

Life Management

For several years I have been leading workshops on how to prevent unwanted stress. My workshops apply the principles of what I call *life management:* directing one's personal lifestyle toward the attainment of physical health, emotional well-being and spiritual contentment. Such health and satisfaction are the fruits of prevention, so I use only the techniques of prevention in my workshops. I find this approach highly successful. It isn't easy to make prevention of unwanted stress a part of life—we have to work at it. Yet most participants in my groups have discovered that the potential benefits are worth whatever effort is necessary to achieve them. This book is my attempt to communicate to a wider audience the process that participants in my workshops have found so rewarding.

My purpose is twofold. My first goal is to develop the insights and understanding necessary to confront unwanted stress in life. However, insights and understanding alone are of little value without the power to put them to work. My second purpose, therefore, is to show how God's power can put us in command of the prevention process. As I develop the factual and logical foundations for the process of stress prevention, I hope I can also help people find, in God's promises, the necessary power to undertake whatever personal changes are required to make the process work.

Before you begin the process, you may wish to learn how stress may be affecting you personally. In figure 1 I have prepared a short self-test to help you estimate the extent to which your personality

---

Figure 1. Stress Profile

Please rate yourself for each of the following characteristics, using a scale of 1 to 5 (5 means that the characteristic describes you very well; 1 means that it does not describe you well at all). Circle the number that represents the degree to which each characteristic describes you.

1. I am never completely satisfied with my accomplishments. 1 2 3 4 5
2. I am very impatient.   1 2 3 4 5
3. People seldom achieve my expectations of them.   1 2 3 4 5
4. I take strong action if I am betrayed, rejected or deceived. 1 2 3 4 5
5. I react strongly to defend myself if I am criticized.   1 2 3 4 5
6. My outlook on life is more serious than that of most
    people.   1 2 3 4 5
7. I am very concerned about what other people think of me. 1 2 3 4 5
8. When important things remain uncertain, I become very
    anxious.   1 2 3 4 5
9. I tend to brood when disappointed or offended.   1 2 3 4 5
10. I find it difficult to relax.   1 2 3 4 5
11. I am often overcome with a sense of hopelessness.   1 2 3 4 5
12. I feel insecure when I am around important, admired and
    accomplished people.   1 2 3 4 5

13.   I am often troubled by feelings of loneliness.   1 2 3 4 5
14.   I feel completely destroyed if I am betrayed, rejected
      or deceived.   1 2 3 4 5

When you have answered all of the questions, transfer each of the numbers you
have circled to the space for the matching question number in one of the two
columns on the following page. Note that several of the questions are represented
in both columns. Add the numbers in each column to get column totals.

Column 1

1. _____

2. _____

3. _____

4. _____

5. _____

6. _____

7. _____

8. _____

9. _____

Total _____

Column 2

6. _____

7. _____

8. _____

9. _____

10. _____

11. _____

12. _____

13. _____

14. _____

Total _____

On the following graph, circle the number range that includes your total for each
column:

		Low Risk			Moderate Risk			High Risk		
Column 1	(A)	9-13	14-17	18-21	22-25	26-29	30-33	34-37	38-41	42-45
Column 2	(P)	9-13	14-17	18-21	22-25	26-29	30-33	34-37	38-41	42-45

Note the risk zone(s) into which each of your scores falls. If both number ranges
you have circled fall within the low-risk zone, and you have answered the questions

honestly, stress is unlikely to cause you health problems. If one or both number ranges fall within one of the higher risk zones, however, stress may contribute to your health risk. If your score in column 1 is higher than your score in column 2, you probably have an "A-type" (active) stress personality; if the reverse is true, you probably have a "P-type" (passive) stress personality.

A-type behavior is characterized by *active* traits such as speed, impatience, aggressiveness and competitive drive. By contrast, P-type behavior is characterized by *passive* traits based on the suppression of personal feelings. Individuals with moderate- or high-risk scores for either A-type or P-type behavior are probably feeling an excessive amount of personal stress and are likely to have higher than normal risk of experiencing certain degenerative diseases.

Scientists must resist trying to group the subjects of their work into nice, neat categories, especially when their work involves human behavior. Like height and weight, behavior tends to follow a continuum with a few individuals at each extreme and most of them grouped together somewhere in the middle. In describing human personality types, it is easy to identify behavior patterns at the extremes of the continuum, but considerably harder to classify behavior that falls in between. For example, most authorities agree on the characteristics of the A-type stress personality. However, although certain personality traits constitute A-type behavior, we cannot always safely say that a particular individual has an A-type personality. Some people strongly express most of the A-type traits. Others express the traits, but with less intensity. Still others exhibit some, but not all, of the traits. All we can do is define a specific pattern of behavior as A-type behavior and then measure how closely an individual's personality fits that defined pattern.

The Stress Profile can help you estimate your tendency toward a particular stress personality. It can warn you of possible health risks that your experience of stress may be creating. But you are a complex individual, and no fourteen-question test can give complete or infallible answers about your personality. The purpose of the Stress Profile is not to predict your future, but only to alert you to possible problems ahead.

---

may increase your risk of stress-related health problems. I developed this simple personality analysis over a number of years, with the cooperation of the participants in my workshops. The Stress Profile began as a rather extensive survey employing more than twice its present number of questions. With continual statistical analysis on a growing body of answers from participants, I discovered that personality trends could be determined with considerable consistency using only the questions I have listed here. To simplify the scoring in this profile, all of the questions had to be given equal weight. My studies suggest that some of the questions are somewhat better indicators of stress personality than others. However, for the goal I hope to achieve here—your awareness of any possible trends—the profile as presented has proved to be quite reliable.

2 What Is Stress?

THE STRESS MYTH EXISTS PRIMARILY BECAUSE THE true meaning of stress has become lost in an abundance of alternative definitions. It's no wonder that people have difficulty understanding what stress is. Every time they turn around, somebody has given it a new meaning.

How do we find the correct definition of stress among all the alternatives at hand? Over the years, I have advised my classes that the correct definition of stress can be found in any physiology textbook. More recently I have had to qualify that statement somewhat. I now say any *good* physiology textbook. It is apparent that even textbook authors can be caught up in a myth. In current practice, the meaning of stress has become almost a matter of opinion. Yet because an understanding of the meaning of stress is so critical to the process of stress prevention, we cannot be satisfied with anything but the true definition.

Should you then accept at face value the definition of stress I am about to offer? Not unless I can justify that definition to your complete satisfaction. In the following chapters I am going to lead you through a process of stress prevention founded on a very specific and unequivocal definition of stress. If you are not satisfied with that definition, the process will do little to help you overcome your unwanted stress.

Here is the definition of stress as it is presented in a textbook of medical physiology:

"ALARM" OR "STRESS" FUNCTION OF THE SYMPATHETIC NERVOUS SYSTEM

. . . mass sympathetic discharge increases in many ways the capability of the body to perform vigorous muscle activity. Let us quickly summarize these ways:

1. Increased arterial pressure
2. Increased blood flow to active muscles concurrent with decreased blood flow to organs that are not needed for rapid activity
3. Increased rates of cellular metabolism throughout the body
4. Increased blood glucose concentration
5. Increased glycolysis in muscles
6. Increased muscle strength
7. Increased mental activity
8. Increased rate of blood coagulation

The sum of these effects permits the person to perform far more strenuous physical activity than would otherwise be possible.

Since it is physical *stress* that usually excites the sympathetic system, it is frequently said that the purpose of the sympathetic system is to provide extra activation of the body in states of stress: This is often called the sympathetic stress *reaction*. (A. C. Guyton, *Basic Human Physiology: Normal Function and Mechanisms of Disease*, 2d ed. [Philadelphia: Saunders, 1977], pp. 600-601.)

This is the definition that I, as a physiologist, consider to be medically correct and historically consistent. However, such a technical description, no matter how correct, is of limited value to the average lay reader unless it can be reduced to more understandable terms and can be practically employed in efforts to overcome the burden of unwanted stress.

In general, what this definition tells us is that stress is not an influence in the world, but a reaction in the body. Today it is common to hear people talk about the stressful circumstances in which they live and work. One person may say her job is full of stress. Another may complain about all the stress he is required to endure at home. But stress does not occur in jobs or in family conflicts. It occurs only within the human body.

Stress is a specific physiological phenomenon with clearly established characteristics recognized by medical scientists for years. To understand how stress works, we first need to know how the human body deals with change. The body strives constantly to maintain stability. No matter what the temperature of its surroundings, for example, a healthy human body will keep its own temperature to within a fraction of a degree of 37° Celsius. It may sweat profusely to overcome the surrounding heat, or it may shiver violently to combat the cold. But it will, if at all possible, preserve its stability.

Stress is part of the army of internal mechanisms the body uses to protect stability. It is a biological response intended to help the body deal with assaults on its status quo. Correctly defined, *stress* is not a cause, but an effect; not an action, but a reaction. In fact, I will speak of the *stress response* to emphasize that stress comes from within, not from without.

When I ask my classes to describe how stress feels, I get a wide variety of answers reflecting the many different ways people experience the stress response. Some terms I hear frequently are *tense, nervous, uptight, irritable, headachy, upset.* Whatever their individual experience, people virtually always agree that stress is physically unpleasant. It is a feeling they would much rather not have.

To understand the nature of stress, we might begin by asking where these unpleasant feelings come from. What is the body doing in its drive to preserve stability? Let's take a look at some specific stress responses and see if we can find some answers.

Fight or Flight

Of the many stress mechanisms at work in the human body, the most familiar are those intended to prepare the body for physical activity. For example, in a typical stress response the heart rate and blood pressure increase, the resistance to blood flow in certain blood vessels lowers, and the blood flow to body tissues not immediately important to physical survival decreases. This all increases the availability of fuel and oxygen to muscles and to the brain. The stress response also involves an increase in muscle tension to prepare for immediate activity and an increase in nerve irritability which decreases reaction time when the situation requires quick response.

All of these are "fight or flight" reactions. That is, their purpose is to preserve life and limb (stability) by preparing the body either to confront or to flee a perceived threat. These stress responses are essential to human survival. For example, imagine Alfred the pioneer in a wagon train surrounded by natives on the warpath. As he crouches behind his wagon, taking quick but careful aim with his rifle, he needs every bit of physical capability he can muster to protect himself and his family members. Alfred's heart rate and blood pressure are elevated, his muscles tense and his nerves on edge. Alfred is under extreme stress. He needs to be, if he hopes to survive.

Thus, stress is not an evil force to be eliminated. It is an essential human survival mechanism. And even if today we do not face life-threatening circumstances as frequently as our pioneer forefathers did, anyone who has ever driven an automobile on modern highways knows that the stress response is still needed to preserve life and limb. Some people complain that they cannot live with their stress, but the fact is that we cannot live without it. That doesn't mean, however, that we must spend our lives enduring all of its potentially unpleasant effects.

Many influences which result in a stress response are not threats to life or even to safety. When a twentieth-century business executive has a bad day at work, he does not face any immediate physical threat. Yet if he chooses to interpret the situation as a major assault on his stability, the biological result will be exactly the same as if he were a pioneer defending against attack. He will experience the same "fight or flight" response: elevated heart rate and blood pressure, increased muscle tension and nerve irritability. His body will be completely prepared to fight hostile warriors. But in his case, the only visible enemy is his overflowing in-basket.

The executive's actual situation has no need—and no outlet— for a physical response. As a result, his body will find alternate outlets for its stress preparations. He will experience those unpleasant sensations that he knows so well and dislikes so much: a throbbing pulse, tense muscles and frayed nerves. Stress, the pioneer's ally, is this executive's enemy, not because it has outlived its usefulness as a survival mechanism, but because modern society has become so adept at abusing it. *If the situation requires no immediate physical reaction, stress is always an inappropriate response.*

What, then, is the appropriate use of the stress response? It is to produce just the amount of stress needed to prepare the body to meet the immediate physical demands of the situation. Any stress in excess of that amount is inappropriate and potentially detrimental. How do we know when our stress level is excessive? We feel it! We become tense, irritable, tired and headachy. But what about the people who claim to work best under stress? Without question, some stress is essential preparation for any kind of work, whether digging ditches or programming computers. Even sit-down intellectual work requires some physical preparation. But that requirement is limited, and the experience of excessive stress typically occurs in such nonphysical situations.

Stress and Responsibility

Some physically inactive work situations demand a high degree of personal responsibility. Air-traffic controllers, for example, are often the subject of public sympathy because of the perceived high-stress nature of their work. The reasoning goes like this: when on duty, air-traffic controllers are under a great deal of pressure because of their continuous responsibility for the lives of thousands of people. For controllers, constant vigilance and attention to detail are essential. This level of alertness requires a perpetual state of stress. Thus, according to this logic, air-traffic controllers have to accept stress-related problems such as nervous breakdowns or family conflict as occupational hazards.

It is important to remember the difference between *stress* and *excess stress*. As we have seen, stress is an essential survival mechanism, whereas excess stress is both unnecessary and potentially harmful. There is no question that air-traffic controllers must remain constantly alert while on the job. Their job, like all jobs, demands a certain amount of stress to prepare the body to meet its specific requirements. But it requires no excess stress! In fact, excess stress can actually impair job performance, both in the short run and in the long run.

In a recent lecture I defined stress as a physical response in the human body, and I pointed out that excess stress can be avoided. Afterward I was approached by a woman who identified herself as an intensive-care nurse. She, like many others I have encountered from "high-stress" professions, argued that her daily experience of unpleasant stress was an unavoidable part of the job. She protested my suggestion that the disagreeable side effects of her work were the consequence of poor stress control rather than inescapable job pressures. When at the end of every shift she returned home in a state of utter physical and emotional collapse, she wanted to believe that her condition was brought on by the "stress" of her work and that she had earned both the collapse and her family's sympathy.

This kind of attitude is not at all uncommon. Not only is it reinforced by the prevailing counsels of contemporary stress researchers; it is also used by some scientists to support their position. The currently dominant viewpoint is based on the work of the eminent stress researcher, the late Dr. Hans Selye (see his *Stress without Distress* [New York: New American Library, 1974]). Selye's theories are based to a great extent on his laboratory observations of rats subjected to various "stressful" conditions. His conclusions have been supported by the fact that the behavior and pathology of humans "under stress" are similar to what he observed in the rats.

Selye defines stress as the body's response to a need for adaptation. The adaptation process, he believes, occurs at the expense of a consumable commodity which he calls "adaptation energy." If we experience a great deal of stress, Selye suggests, we can run out of this adaptation energy—and then we become "stress exhausted." In such a condition, according to Selye, we are highly susceptible to disease.

There is no question that laboratory rats adapt in the manner just described, and it seems clear that they experience exhaustion when they are forced to continue adapting for extended periods. There is also no question that both the air-traffic controller and the intensive-care nurse experience a similar kind of exhaustion after they have been at work for many hours. But the question is whether, in humans, this reaction is as unavoidable as it is in rats.

Laboratory rats have contributed a great deal to scientific understanding, and I have often used them in my work. But rats are not identical to humans, and one must use caution in applying to people conclusions based on rats. In this case, I think the comparison has been extended well beyond its usefulness. To base a theory of human stress on rodent behavior is to assume parallels where none may exist. Just because people frequently behave like rats doesn't mean they have no other options.

The conditions to which the rats are exposed in such experiments are not common in modern human experience. Rats do not worry about money, time pressures or how their children are going to turn out, so the "stresses" imposed in the laboratory must be primarily physical—temperature changes, physical trauma, food deprivation. By contrast, little human stress in our society results from such direct assaults. Rather, most of what we know as stress arises in response to nonphysical threats or perceived dangers. Thus the experimental conditions used with the rats do not apply.

A Matter of Choice

Humans can decide how they wish to react to their circumstances. The fact that we frequently choose to act like laboratory rats does not make us the same as rats. Unfortunately, we so often choose to behave like rats that it sometimes looks as if we have no more control over stress than they do. Yet the fact remains—we have the choice. We can, if we wish, choose not to be like rats.

For example, the intensive-care nurse frequently experienced stress exhaustion while working. She concluded that, like a laboratory rat, she was powerless to escape the unpleasant effects of her environment. She was a victim of stress exhaustion. Unfortunately, a lot of people involved in stress research and stress education have adopted a similar viewpoint.* I believe this

*See, for example, any of the following references:
Herbert Benson, *The Relaxation Response* (New York: Avon Books, 1975).
Barbara R. Brown, *Stress and the Art of Biofeedback* (New York: Bantam Books, 1977).
Gary R. Collins, *Spotlight on Stress* (Ventura, Calif.: Vision House, 1982).
John J. Parrino, *From Panic to Power* (New York: Wiley, 1977).
Kenneth R. Pelletier, *Mind as Healer, Mind as Slayer* (New York: Delta Books, 1977).
Charles F. Stroebel, *QR: The Quieting Reflex* (New York: Berkeley Books, 1982).

viewpoint misjudges the role of personal choice in creating unwanted stress and ignores the human's ability to make choices that are more perceptive than those made by a rat.

I have an experimental basis for concluding that human stress exhaustion, in most cases, occurs as a matter of choice rather than as a matter of fate. Although the intensive-care nurse claimed the right to be stress exhausted after a single eight-hour shift at the hospital, I have seen people under extreme stress for ten to twelve hours a day, seven days a week, who showed not the slightest hint of stress exhaustion. These people, runners in a transcontinental road race, ran forty to seventy miles a day every day for weeks. While running they experienced great increases in heart rate, blood pressure, muscle tension and all the other stress indicators. Why were they not stress exhausted? Because they needed all of the stress to accomplish their physical goals. They had no excess stress. Of course they were physically tired at the end of each day, but we must be careful to make the clear distinction between simple physical exhaustion and stress exhaustion. Simple physical exhaustion occurs when we direct stress to meet the legitimate physical needs of the body. Stress exhaustion occurs when we continually misdirect stress to physically stimulate a body that doesn't need it and can't use it.

Any kind of physical activity requires a stress response. There is no essential difference between the response required for the wide receiver in football to escape the clutches of the defensive back and the response required for the pioneer to escape the scalping knife. And in both cases, the stress response is no different from that of the air-traffic controller sitting at his console in the control center. The difference is that the football player and the pioneer need all their stress; the air-traffic controller generally does not. An athlete typically produces just enough stress to meet the physical needs of the immediate situation. Under such circumstances, there is no excess stress. Only excess stress is experienced as unpleasant and unwanted, and only excess stress causes stress exhaustion. Whenever the stress response is appropriate to the body's physical needs, there is no excess stress and no stress exhaustion. And we can learn to choose a stress response that will not exceed our needs. That is the subject of the rest of this book.

3 Interpreting Our World

SOME STRESS IS A CONSCIOUS RESPONSE TO A SITUATION that is interpreted as dangerous and demanding action. When Alfred the pioneer saw hostile natives, he correctly interpreted the situation as a threat to his survival and reacted with stress to prepare himself to confront it. The frustrated executive also interpreted his situation as a threat, but his stress response exceeded his body's needs in the circumstances. Both Alfred and the executive reacted to their situations with an *interpretive stress response*.

Not all stress responses result from such conscious interpretations of life situations. Some stress is a normal result of the body's need to maintain biological stability. This kind of stress response occurs whenever the body has to adapt to changes in its surroundings or to adjustments in its chemical balance. When the environmental temperature changes, for example, the body adapts to preserve a constant internal temperature. This adaptation does not happen by conscious choice, but by necessity. It is an *adaptive stress response.* Because of their critical role in maintaining biological stability, most adaptive stress responses cannot and should not be prevented. (See appendixes C and D for a detailed description of two exceptions to this rule—adaptive stress responses caused by certain common drugs or by food intake that upsets the body's fuel economy.)

But most people, when they use the word *stress,* are not talking about their normal, necessary adaptive stress responses. Instead they are talking about interpretive stress responses, and they are probably not looking at the responses so much as at specific events, circumstances or relationships that they think caused their stress. The process which leads to an interpretive stress response follows a set pathway. Figure 2 shows how external circumstances come to be perceived as stress.

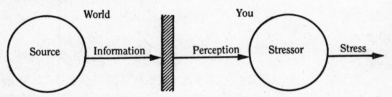

Figure 2.   The Interpretive Stress Response

The two domains identified in this diagram, the *world* and *you,* are separated by a distinct barrier. The only communication between the two domains is the flow of information in the direction shown. It is important to remember that the two elements in circles, the *source* and the *stressor,* always remain within their respective domains.

The chain of events leading to an interpretive stress response is set off by a *source* in the external world. The source sends out *information* about itself. You *perceive* this information and interpret it according to your past experience. You may see the source as frightening, inviting, pleasurable, painful, challenging or irrelevant. If you perceive the source as a threat to your stability, you will identify it as a *stressor*. (Note that the stressor exists in you and not in the world.) Whenever a stressor exists in you, you will experience *stress* which prepares your body to deal with the perceived threat.

Imagine, for example, that while walking down the street you look up and discover that a car has just jumped the curb and is heading straight for you. The *source,* the oncoming car, is sending *information* about its velocity and mass. By means of *perception* based on experience, you interpret the hurtling car to be a *stressor,* or threat. As a result, you experience *stress*. Your body is immediately equipped to react—to jump out of the way. This is clearly an appropriate stress response. It achieves the result that stress is intended to accomplish—your survival.

However, not all stress responses are appropriate, because not all stress is needed for survival. To see how unwanted and potentially harmful stress occurs, we need to look more closely at the source, the stressor and perception.

The Source Is Not the Stressor

In interpretive stress responses, the *source* is external. It exists only in the world. It can be a person, a situation, an object, or anything else with identifiable characteristics. It is not the source of stress, but of information. It becomes part of the stress initiation process only if it is perceived in certain ways.

The *stressor* is the actual cause of the interpretive stress response. It does not exist in the external world; it is not the same as the source. It is what you believe the source to be. As the product of your perception of the source, it exists only in you. It is built solely on your interpretation. Without the stressor, there will be no interpretive stress response. Once the stressor exists, a stress response will always follow.

Perception is as individual as a fingerprint, for all perception is based in the observer's experience. Because no two people ever have identical experiences, their perceptions of the same source will always differ—perhaps slightly, perhaps to a great degree. Thus the intrinsic nature of the source does not initiate stress, but rather the individual's perception of it. A source that is identified as a stressor promotes a stress response; the same source, if it is not perceived as a stressor, does not initiate stress. In the dynamics of interpretive stress responses, reality is only what it is perceived to be.

For example, I find among the people attending my workshops a variety of opinions about the virtues of snakes. When I ask them to predict their reactions if I were to release a small and completely harmless reptile in the middle of the classroom, I get extremely varied responses. Some acknowledge that the event would cause them severe anxiety. Others say that the creature's presence would stimulate little more than curiosity. Some participants, then, would react with stress while others would hardly react at all. Both groups would be observing the same source. Why would it provoke stress in some but not in others? The difference is in their individual perceptions. The fact that a snake is loose in the room is simply information. The people's reactions would not be based on the information itself, but on their interpretations of it.

An interpretive stress response, like an adaptive stress response, is produced to preserve or restore stability. In some cases, the threat to stability is clear and the resulting stress response is appropriate. If the source is accurately perceived as a real threat to survival— for example, an out-of-control automobile plunging toward a pedestrian—a stress response is essential to prepare the body to meet the threat.

Often, however, the source does not actually threaten immediate physical survival, and yet the person produces just as great a stress response as if real danger existed. In such cases, the existence or magnitude of the threat is perceived incorrectly, giving rise to stress for which the body has no need and no appropriate outlet. In the process of finding some outlet for this excess stress, the body undergoes a variety of reactions that cause discomfort and, in some cases, disease. For example, a father waits for his sometimes rebellious teen-aged daughter to come home after a party. Her curfew is midnight. At 12:10, he notices a headache coming on. At 12:20, he begins to feel jumpy and irritable. At 12:30, his pulse starts to race. On the one hand, he fears for her safety. On the other, he dreads the confrontation they will have if she is simply ignoring the house rules. "I can't live with this constant stress," he complains to his wife, blaming his daughter's behavior for his physical symptoms. And yet his situation calls for no immediate physical response. His stress response, since it is inappropriate to the immediate physical requirements of the circumstances, is entirely unnecessary.

Certainly the father is right to care about his daughter's safety as well as for her respect of house rules. But a stress response does not advance either one of these concerns. One set of actions is available for how he should deal with his daughter. Another is available for how he should deal with his stress. The latter is the concern of this book.

If excess stress is unwanted, unpleasant and potentially harmful to health, why do we produce it in the first place? Many people think stress is unavoidable because the "stressful" circumstances of their lives cannot be prevented. In other words, like the intensive-care nurse who blamed her job for her constant stress, they accuse various external sources of being stressors. But as we have seen, stressors never exist in the external *world.* They exist only in *you,* and then only as a result of perception. Unwanted stress is not the fault of the source; it is the fault of incorrect interpretation. This fact is central to our understanding of stress and stress prevention. It is summarized in the first two of what I am fond of calling Ecker's Laws:

Ecker's First Law: *If the stress is unwanted and unpleasant, it is always excessive to the physical needs of the circumstances.*

Ecker's Second Law: *If the stress response is greater than the need, the perception is always wrong.*

Changing Faulty Perceptions

Given, then, that unneeded and unwanted stress is the product of faulty perception, it should be clear that any effort we make to prevent unnecessary stress must be centered on changing our perceptions. Of course, it is sometimes appropriate to attempt to alter the situation—to solve money problems by finding a job, to improve grades by studying harder, to feel healthier by eating more wisely—but not as a means of eliminating excess stress. Although promoting changes in the external environment can at times be important, that is not the topic I am dealing with. Rather it is how we can prevent unwanted stress whether the situation improves, deteriorates or stays about the same. I am concerned with perceptions, not situations. But before we can change our perceptions, we need to understand something about their origins and how they can cause us to produce stress responses in nonthreatening situations.

Perceptions are based on our past. They are built on everything we were, are and hope to be. If our perceptions give rise to unnecessary stress responses, it means that some of our views of reality are faulty. That is, some sources in the world which we perceive as threats to survival are, in reality, completely neutral. The father who suffered intense stress because his daughter was half an hour late had a faulty concept of reality. In his situation, no physical response was necessary or even useful. His inappropriate response indicated that he was not accepting this reality.

The human body produces the stress response solely to deal with instability. Even in cases of inappropriate stress, the individual feels that something in his or her life is in danger of becoming unstable. In most such cases the situation poses no threat to the person's physical stability. But there is more to life than the physical dimension. Humans also have an emotional dimension that can be endangered, and emotional threats can cause inappropriate stress. What elements of the emotional structure are capable of being threatened? How do such threats occur? Why do we prepare ourselves to respond to these nonphysical threats with stress, a purely physical reaction?

The Stability Structure

To help answer these questions, let us consider what I call the *stability structure*. As part of normal human development, every individual develops a set of beliefs about the world and guiding principles for living in it. We use these principles to ensure emotional stability when our lives are subjected to uncertainty or threatened with loss of control. "Mother feeds me." "Stoves are hot." "Barking dogs sometimes bite." "Ambitious people succeed." "Love your enemies." These beliefs and principles are rarely articulated, and few people are conscious of them. Yet they provide the basis for our self-concept and our perceptions of the surrounding world. In effect, they provide the stability structure that holds our lives together.

Stability is freedom from the influence of change. As we discussed in an earlier chapter, the human body craves biological stability. Similarly, emotional stability is a universal human need. It, however, is harder to define than biological stability; and whatever it is, it clearly is not experienced in exactly the same way by all people.

In general, emotional stability exists when the stability structure keeps the individual from being adversely affected—changed for the worse—by potentially disturbing external influences. For example, many people see the fortieth birthday as a major transition point. Whether or not the event will be emotionally upsetting depends solely on the strength of the individual's stability structure. People whose structures are built on satisfaction with who they are will see their fortieth birthday as a nonthreatening milestone, whereas people who are dissatisfied with themselves or who fear growing older may feel threatened by the prospect of entering middle age.

Change, of course, is an inevitable fact of life. We cannot stop the clock, control nature or regulate the attitudes and activities of everyone whose lives touch ours. Another fact of life is equally clear—the human body's stress-initiating mechanisms cannot distinguish between threats to physical stability and threats to emotional stability. Stress is the tool the body uses to combat instability, whatever its origin. If change causes us emotional instability, the onset of unwanted and unnecessary stress is inevitable. Obviously, then, the only way to prevent unwanted stress is to improve the way our stability structures deal with change.

Suppose I need to build and occupy a watchtower in an area that is often buffeted by high winds. I can build the tower with a flimsy support structure and hope it won't be unstable when the wind blows. Then when the storms come I can curse the winds for causing the instability I am required to endure. On the other hand, I can either build my tower with a strong support base or reinforce my weak tower so that no matter how hard the wind blows, the tower will continue to be stable. The wind—change or threat of change—will always be with us. The only way to ensure stability—freedom from stress—is to build a strong stability structure in the first place, or to reinforce the weak structure I already have.

Unlike my biological structure, which came into existence without any contribution on my part, my stability structure is a product of my own creation. Of course many principles and ideals which contribute to my stability structure come from outside sources: parents, teachers, churches, the media, friends. But they remain a part of my structure by my personal decision. For example, Mary's mother raised her to see financial security as one of life's highest goals. This principle has become the keystone in Mary's stability structure. As a result, she is now constantly concerned about the adequacy of her income, and even minor financial setbacks cause her severe stress. Her stability structure is not equipped to protect her from changes in financial status. She perceives such changes as stressors—threats to her stability—and they always provoke in her an unwanted and unpleasant stress response. She does not have to view life in that way; she chooses to do so. The principle may have originally been her mother's, but it's hers now, and it will stay with her until she decides she doesn't want it any longer.

Like a biological change, an emotional change may pose a threat to survival—but it is not a physical threat. Rather, it is a threat to the self-image and to the stability structure that preserves and protects it. Stress, a physical response, cannot protect us against an emotional threat, but that doesn't stop us from being stressed when we perceive that our self-image is in danger.

When I tell participants in my workshops that unwanted stress is caused by a faulty self-image, someone nearly always protests, "I have a lot of problems with stress, but my self-image is great. My stress can't be caused by a faulty self-image." Most of us don't like to acknowledge that our self-image is anything short of perfect, but many of us have lost touch with our real identity or are hesitant to inspect it critically. The fact is that if our self-image were as solid as we'd like to believe, we wouldn't perceive external events as threats to our emotional stability, and we wouldn't meet them with a stress response.

Self-Image and the Spiritual Nature
In describing human nature I have thus far identified two distinct aspects—the physical and the emotional. But there is another side to human existence, important in understanding self-image—the spiritual. My spiritual nature grows out of my belief or faith in certain ideas, values and standards. My self-concept is based on that belief system. When I declare "I'm somebody"—that is, I have value as a human life—or "I'm nobody," I am not stating a fact or even

a hypothesis. I am simply expressing my belief, a matter of faith. Self-image, as its name suggests, is an image or concept of who I am. It is a constructed identity that exists only as long as I choose for it to exist and in whatever form I want it to have. My self-image reflects what I believe myself to be—nothing more, nothing less. Self-image is a matter of faith, not fact.

Self-image, however, is not an isolated element in my belief system. It influences and is influenced by all the other elements that form the foundations of my faith. If these elements give little support to my self-concept, my identity is likely to be tenuous and easily controlled by outside influences. On the other hand, if the foundations of my faith provide a solid, authoritative basis for my self-image, my identity will be highly resistant to such control. For Christians, personal identity is based on the belief that they are created in the image of God. Self-worth then becomes much more than a matter of personal conviction—it is a matter of divine promise.

Christians then have an advantage in dealing with unwanted stress. Even so, the faithful are not automatically guaranteed freedom from stress. In fact, the history of God's people includes many examples of believers who did not handle difficult situations well. Abraham, already in possession of God's promise to make of him a great nation, tried to pass his wife off as his sister because he feared that "they will kill me because of my wife" (Gen 20:11). In spite of continual miracles showing God's guidance during the exodus, the children of Israel poured forth a steady stream of stress-motivated complaints. Peter, after three years of working with Jesus, denied association with him because he feared the consequences.

On the other hand, Scripture also abounds in accounts of those faithful who were able to maintain a proper perspective of their God-given identities and to prevent problems from altering that perspective. Moses, with God's promises echoing in his memory, fearlessly confronted the king of Egypt and presented his demands for the release of God's people. Ezra, unwilling to deny God's power by asking Artaxerxes for an armed escort to protect his band of Hebrew expatriates as they returned to Israel from exile, journeyed some five hundred miles over hostile terrain in complete confidence. Peter, the trial-night coward, later stood before the Jewish council and proclaimed without equivocating: "We must obey God rather than men" (Acts 5:29).

What made the difference between the believers who were overcome by stress and those who faced difficult situations unafraid? Their willingness to identify with—to base their self-image on—God and his purposes. Peter abandoned that identity in the high priest's courtyard, but recovered it as he began working to establish the church. Like Peter before Pentecost, we often abandon our identification with God and become captive to self-made identities and the unwanted stress that these poorly grounded identities inevitably engender. Fortunately, we don't have to remain captive. As we progress through the stress-prevention process, we will learn how to face the world with confidence, free of stress and assured of our God-given identities.

4 Analyzing Stress

*W*HEN MEDICAL STUDENTS ENTER THE PRACTICAL phase of training to be physicians, one of the first techniques they learn is the process of diagnosis. Through physical examination and laboratory tests, they learn to pinpoint the cause of a patient's condition before appropriate therapy can begin. Preventing unwanted stress involves a similar process, one that I call *stress analysis*. Stress analysis is a diagnostic tool you can use to identify the origins of stress reactions in other people and in yourself. As you will soon discover, clearly identifying the origins of unwanted stress is absolutely essential to successful stress elimination and prevention.

To lay a foundation for our study of stress analysis and stress prevention, I illustrate in figure 3 the relationship between your internal stability structure and an external reality that may threaten it. Notice that the square, representing your stability structure, is made up of several geometric figures, representing the various elements of your personal identity. The open space in the center is the area that your present self-image allows for your perception of the specific external reality called A. Stability is maintained as long as all of the geometric elements fit within the perimeters of the square.

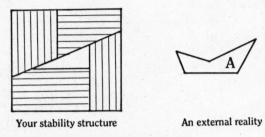

Your stability structure   An external reality

Figure 3.   A Stability Structure and an External Reality

Obviously A, the indicated external reality, cannot be accommodated in your present stability structure. There just isn't room for it. If you try to force it into the open space in the center, the rest of the geometric figures will be upset. The elements of your personal identity will no longer fit neatly into your stability structure. The result, as figure 4 shows, is instability. The body will deal with this instability by provoking a stress response.

One way to integrate A into your stability structure is to leave the

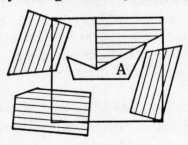

Figure 4.   Upsetting a Stability Structure

elements of the structure alone and try to change A. As an external reality, A is very difficult to change. Attempts to do so, which we will discuss as "stress-motivated behavior," are seldom successful.

If A can't be changed, however, it can be denied. You can re-create it as a fantasy. The real A won't fit into your present stability structure without causing instability, but your fantasy of A can be accommodated quite easily if you make it the same shape as your open space (see figure 5). For example, Bill and Ned occupy equivalent lower-management positions in a large corporation. They are in competition for promotion to the next management level. Ned is highly competent, self-assured and well-liked. Bill cannot accept this reality in his competitor—it cannot be accommodated in his structure without creating instability (diminished self-image). So Bill generates a fantasy of a flawed Ned with such attributes as being "stuck up" and "toady" to permit the existence of Ned to be comfortably accommodated in his stability structure.

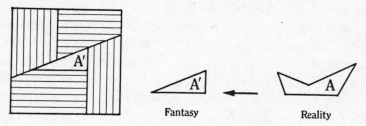

Figure 5. Creating a Fantasy to Maintain Stability

Of course, this solution has problems of its own. Except for people who are so emotionally unstable that they cannot identify reality, everyone has to face the moment of truth sometime. And when that happens, the fantasy will disappear and the structure will again be thrown into instability. Denying the reality of A and changing it to suit your needs provide no lasting solutions to unwanted stress.

It should be apparent by now that the only way to integrate the real A into your stability structure is for *you* to change—to alter the elements of your structure so that A can be accommodated in it, as in figure 6. In practical terms, this means you must change your concept of self. We will discuss such changes in more detail in a later chapter.

Figure 6. *Changing a Stability Structure to Accommodate a New Reality*

Stress-Motivated Behavior

People who attend my workshops say that they have come to learn how to deal with stress because it is a problem for them. They don't like what they experience, and they want to get rid of it. I have yet to meet anyone who claims to enjoy the feelings an excess stress response provokes. When you consider the pervasiveness of stress-related problems in our world, it is not hard to believe that much human behavior is an attempt to deal with stress. Typically, people who experience unpleasant physical sensations try to eliminate the discomfort. As Ogden Nash observed,

There was a young belle of old Natchez

Whose garments were always in patchez.

When comment arose

On the state of her clothes,

She drawled, When Ah itchez, Ah scratchez!

(*The Face Is Familiar: The Selected Verse of Ogden Nash* [Garden City, N.Y.: Garden City Publishing Co., 1941], p. 341. Reprinted by arrangement with Little, Brown & Co.) When we itch, we scratch. When we have a headache, we take aspirin. When we have indigestion, we take antacids. In the same way, when we experience the unpleasant consequences of excess stress, we try to relieve them. Anyone who has suffered from migraine headaches, chronic allergies or nagging arthritis can testify to the extreme measures people will use to achieve relief.

Why do we take aspirin when we have a headache? Because informed sources tell us that aspirin will alleviate pain. What do informed sources tell us about eliminating the discomfort of unwanted stress? Advocates of intervention therapy advise us to learn relaxation techniques and to increase physical activity to give outlet to the excess stress. Such advice is based on the belief that excess stress is unavoidable, that the world is full of stressors over which we have no control.

Interventionists have identified a number of alleged stressors and have rated them according to how much stress they can be expected to provoke. The Social Readjustment Rating Scale, a list of stress-producing life situations, has become a popular self-evaluation test (see T. H. Holmes and R. H. Rahe, "The Social Readjustment Rating Scale," *Psychosomatic Research* 11 [1967]: 213). It is frequently quoted in magazine articles and is even used as a party game. On a scale of 1 to 100, the SRRS gives a stress value to each of a variety of common events. The value assigned is supposed to be the relative amount of stress that a person could expect to suffer as a result of experiencing the event. For example, on this rating scale the death of a spouse has a value of 100; loss of employment, 47; trouble with in-laws, 29; and a traffic violation, 11.

I call the SRRS the Permission Slip. It justifies an experience of stress in the listed situations by identifying them as universal and unavoidable stressors. It gives us permission to have a certain amount of stress any time we undergo one of the events. But permission is not what we need. Stress does not feel more comfortable just because some document authorizes it. Neither is it eliminated nor are any of its unpleasant effects moderated.

The most serious problem with the SRRS is not that it is worthless in helping people deal with their stress, but that it perpetuates the myth that certain events are inevitably stressors and that we are powerless to avoid stress when these events occur in our lives. Thus it reinforces the common belief that the only way to prevent stress is to eliminate or escape its source. The resulting efforts to neutralize the source in order to control the stress are what I call *stress-motivated behavior.*

Attending a workshop several years ago was a middle-aged couple whom I shall call Bob and Darlene. Bob was a vocal fellow who openly acknowledged a life full of problems which caused him considerable stress. Not the least of his problems was Darlene, whom he described accurately as a high-stress personality. She had already experienced two heart attacks, but, according to Bob, she refused to slow down. Yet unlike her husband, Darlene remained as inconspicuous as possible in class and said nothing.

During the first two sessions, whenever I made a point that Bob felt supported his opinion about Darlene's need to change her lifestyle, he gave her a quick jab in the ribs and whispered so everyone could hear, "Did you get that?" In the third session, concerned for the abuse being suffered by Darlene's rib cage, I asked Bob to sit on the other side of the room. But that didn't slow Bob down. Thereafter, whenever my explanations struck a responsive chord in Bob, he jabbed his finger in Darlene's direction in mock concealment behind his other hand.

In the sixth and final session, I confronted Bob with his behavior and asked if he had been listening enough in class to understand what he was doing. My question left him surprised and perplexed. Every other participant in the group knew exactly what he was doing and why. But he had been too busy with his own stress-motivated behavior to listen even to a discussion of how to eliminate stress.

Bob protested that his behavior had a commendable motivation—

concern for Darlene's health and welfare. But the rest of us recognized that his concern for her was secondary to his need to control his own stress. Darlene's condition was not helped by the rib poking and finger pointing. In fact, since Darlene was a private person who became stressed herself when she was subjected to public attention, her condition was significantly aggravated by her husband's antics. Bob wanted her to change her ways so she would not die and leave him alone. The stress he felt as a result of this fear caused him to engage in behavior that actually increased the threat to her life.

Behavior like Bob's is not at all uncommon. And, like Bob, most people will claim vehemently that their motivation is not to relieve personal stress, but rather to help others or to establish justice. For example, who hasn't at one time or another given someone a perfect squelch, a masterful put-down? Why do we do it? We usually answer, "He had it coming." But is this the real reason? Nobody elected us judge and jury to put him in his proper place, and nobody is going to benefit from his being squelched. We are not establishing justice so much as neutralizing an existing or potential source of personal stress. If we are "one up" on the other guy, his possible threat to our stability becomes a little less significant.

Games and Manipulation

Stress-motivated behavior has one purpose, though it is seldom recognized and never admitted. That purpose is to eliminate stress. It employs a single strategy—to force a change in the source. These two properties, ulterior motive and manipulative strategy, were pointed out by the late Eric Berne, originator of transactional analysis, in his book *Games People Play* (New York: Grove Press, 1964). Playing manipulative "games" is the most common technique used in our society to deal with stress. But games have two significant qualities we need to bear in mind. First, they virtually never produce a lasting solution; that is, they do not get rid of the cause of the stress. Second, they are almost always destructive in outcome.

Take the situation with Bob and Darlene. Bob was playing a game with his wife. His professed purpose was to preserve her health, but his ulterior motive was to control his own stress. His strategy was to use the authority of my remarks and the pressure of the public setting to get her to change into what he wanted her to be—a calm, relaxed, healthy person. But his strategy failed. She was not less anxious as a result of his game; in fact, she was more anxious. His own stress, therefore, did not decrease; it increased.

The basic fault in Bob's reasoning was his belief that Darlene was responsible for his stress. Essentially he was saying, "If she would just shape up, I could stop feeling uptight. If she would just be what I want her to be, my life would be so much easier." But Darlene was not responsible for Bob's stress. She was the *source,* but the source is never the *stressor.* Bob was stressed because of his *perception* of the source. Because he perceived Darlene's poor health as a potential threat to his stability, that perception created a stressor *in him.* Bob did not recognize his own responsibility for his perception, and he determined that only a change in Darlene would preserve his stability. Thus he set about to change her—at any cost.

Bob's game with Darlene followed the fundamental pattern of the universal stress-control game: to relieve stress by forcing a change in the source. The pattern is the same whether the players are young or old, rich or poor, male or female; whether the circumstances involve family or business or school; whether the target of manipulation is a person or an institution or a situation. Here are some examples to show how the game is played:

At a cocktail party, Mr. Ace boasts loudly about his exceptional success in several business deals. Mrs. Ace makes sure the group also hears about some of his more notable failures. Why? Because Mr. Ace's boastful behavior is an embarrassment, a source of stress for her. The only way she knows how to get rid of her uncomfortableness and her stress is to get him to modify his behavior.

Andy Bright, a high-school junior, is scheduled to give an oral report in English class. He has spent little time preparing and fears he will not do well. He arranges to be "sick" and stays home from school. Why? Because the situation at school is a source of stress for him, and the only way he knows to avoid the stress is to avoid the situation.

Mr. Craven owns a small business. On his office door, where everyone in the firm can see it, he has placed a sign which reads: "The BOSS may not always be right . . . but the BOSS is always the BOSS!" Why? Because any challenge to his authority is a source of stress for Mr. Craven, and the only way he knows to avoid the stress is to decrease the possibility of challenge.

Stress-motivated behavior, whatever form it takes, is an attempt to retain or regain control. Mrs. Ace had no direct control over her husband's boasting, so she put him down publicly; Andy Bright had no control over his English assignment, so he skipped class; Mr. Craven feared he would lose control over his employees, so he hung a warning sign. All three were playing manipulative games. But games do not work. They do not help the players gain control. In fact, they often backfire.

Look again at Mr. and Mrs. Ace. She plays a game to gain control over his behavior. But how much control can she achieve? Only as much as he is willing to give up. She can persuade, beg, seduce, or demand—but he alone determines his behavior. In a specific situation, she squelches him enough to cause a temporary end to his boasting, but this does not solve her problem. Mr. Ace, who does not enjoy public put-downs, has his own inappropriate stress response—he does a slow burn for the rest of the evening. This response does not feel good, so he is motivated to find a way to stop it. We can expect him to blame his stress on his wife's "uncalled for" remarks. He will see the solution of his stress problem in terms of some "badly needed" changes in *her* behavior. In other words, he will come up with his own manipulative game and will spend the rest of the evening working out his game plan.

World War 3
In the car on the way home, World War 3 will erupt. World War 3 is a game played by two people under stress. Each blames the other for the stress and tries to manipulate the other into a behavior change. Each is trying to regain lost control, and each sees the other as the cause of that loss. Each is essentially saying, "If you would only be the way I want you to be, I could be back in control and my stress would go away."

Neither player, however, is able to hear what the other is saying, because both are too busy with their own agendas—efforts to eliminate their own stress by any means necessary. Thus, as the game gets into full swing, voices are raised and gestures grow animated. The words *always* and *never* are tossed back and forth. Long-dormant sins are resurrected and used as ammunition. Each barb hurled by Mr. Ace increases Mrs. Ace's stress level and hardens her resolve to neutralize the perceived source of her stress—Mr. Ace. She responds in kind, and on it goes.

The kind of behavior typified by Mr. and Mrs. Ace's World War 3 is common in our society. Manipulative games vary, of course: some people prefer silence to uproar, and still others use subtle innuendoes. But whatever the strategy chosen to deal with it, excess stress remains a powerful force. It can motivate behavior that would ordinarily be considered unthinkable. It can divide families into warring camps, turn businesses into battlegrounds, and even persuade nations to prepare to destroy each other. It tends to be self-perpetuating. As Ecker's Third Law says: *Excess stress promotes excess stress.*

When interpersonal relations degenerate, as in the case of Mr. and Mrs. Ace, misunderstandings multiply. Each game-player believes that the other person has malicious intent; that is, he or she just wants to be mean. It is easy to see how this belief arises. Put yourself in Mr. Ace's shoes. There you are, doing a little harmless bragging at a friendly cocktail party, when this lady—supposedly your friend and helpmate—comes up and tries to make you look like a moron. What are you supposed to think about her action? What possible reason could she have for doing such a thing except downright cussedness? Or think how Mrs. Ace felt during World War 3 on the way home when Mr. Ace sneeringly reminded her about the time she left the car out of gear and it backed down the driveway into a police car. What besides plain meanness could have prompted him to dig up that long-forgotten event?

The answer is that stress, not malice, motivated those unkind actions. Their primary intent was not to hurt the other person, but to preserve personal stability and avoid the unpleasantness of excess stress. They are fundamentally survival reactions.

Consider the following comparative illustration. A lifesaver at a swimming pool has to be able to deal with a drowning person efficiently and dispassionately. A drowning person has only one interest—survival. He will cling to anything that might keep him from going down for the last time. An unwary lifesaver who gets too close to him can become the victim of a viselike stranglehold which puts his own life in danger. But should a lifesaver assume the drowning person is being malicious because, in a frantic effort to survive, he jeopardizes the lifesaver's safety? Of course not. His only intent is survival. It's the same with a person engaged in stress-motivated behavior. The intent of the behavior is not malice but the elimination of unwanted stress.

Mrs. Ace's motive, like a drowning person's, was survival. She perceived her husband's loud boasting as a threat to her emotional stability. This in turn provoked a physical stress response, for the body equates maintenance of stability with survival. Therefore, even though no threat to her physical survival existed, Mrs. Ace's body prepared her to fight for her life. Naturally, the resulting stress, since it had no appropriate outlet, felt extremely unpleasant, and Mrs. Ace wanted to get rid of it. She then turned on her husband, not because she hated him, but in order to restore her own equilibrium.

Understanding the motivation behind bad actions in no way excuses them, but it can make it easier for you to respond to them without invoking your own stress response. Once you have learned to recognize and accept the motivations behind manipulative game playing, you will have taken a giant step toward stress prevention. Like a lifesaver dealing with a drowning person, you will be able to acknowledge that survival, not malice, is the driving force behind such behavior, and you will be able to base your reaction on the action's motive rather than on its wisdom.

A Plea for Power

Fundamentally, stress-motivated behavior is a plea for control. The stressed individual sends this message to the perceived stressor: "I'm under stress, and it's your fault. Stop being what you are so I can stop reacting to you the way I do." In other words, please give me the power to control you.

Every one of us at one time or another has said to someone, "You make me mad!" In essence this means, "You have the power to control my feelings." Where did this person get that kind of power over you? You gave it to him.

When people say to us, "You make me mad" or "You make me feel guilty" or "You make me disgusted" or even "You make me happy," they are granting us a gift—the power to control their emotions. For example, Mr. Popp has a problem employee, Mr. Fish. Mr. Fish tends to take four-martini lunch breaks, significantly decreasing his afternoon work performance. Whenever this happens, Mr. Popp becomes angry, calls Mr. Fish into his office, gives him a tongue-lashing, and then spends the rest of the day stewing about it. As a result, his own work performance suffers too. Who has the power in this situation? Mr. Fish. All he has to do is toss down a few drinks at lunch and he can ruin the rest of his boss's day. Where does he get that kind of power? The boss gives it to him.

Mrs. Trim's four-year-old, Jeff, has a fondness for exploration. Frequently he returns from his neighborhood safaris bruised and dirty, his clothes in tatters. Inevitably Mrs. Trim screams, "Jeffrey! You make me so mad!" and applies a few vengeful swats to his backside. Later, with Jeff crying in his room, Mrs. Trim regrets her outburst and says to herself, "If he just wouldn't provoke me so." Who has the power in this situation? Jeff. Where did he get it? From Mom.

Interestingly, neither Mr. Fish nor Jeff is aware that he possesses power. Each is following his own agenda without thinking about the consequences of his actions. It is doubtful, in fact, that either one of them even wants such power or would know what to do with it if he knew he had it. The characteristics of power distribution in human relationships are described as follows:

Ecker's Fourth Law: *Power to control feelings is never taken; it is only given away.*

Ecker's Fifth Law: *When you give away power, the other person never becomes more powerful—but you always become more powerless.*

One of my workshops was attended by a man who continually complained that he was the victim of powers beyond his control. He constantly encountered intimidators, he said, who would not allow him to function efficiently at work or at home. I replied that there is no such thing as an intimidator. There are only people who make themselves available to be intimidated. This man was not the victim of forces beyond his control. He was the victim of his own powerlessness. If he felt intimidated, it was because he gave to others the power to control his emotions. No one forced that decision on him; this was the way he chose to act.

No one can make us feel intimidated. No one can make us feel guilty. We feel that way because we choose to do so, and we make that choice when we elect to give up the power to feel otherwise. What if, in the face of a situation I have always interpreted as intimidating, I decided to feel confident, cheerful and patient? Now who would have the power? I would. I have always had it, but I previously chose to give it away. What if, instead of becoming angry, Mr. Popp and Mrs. Trim chose to stay calm and deal with their situations in an effective manner? They would retain the power, and Mr. Fish and Jeff would know it.

Strangely enough, people tend to give away power because they hope to gain control. They feel that circumstances are threatening their stability, so they look for ways to control the circumstances. In their effort to control some source that they perceive as threatening, they abandon control of their own emotions. Thus they give up the control they do have—control of their own feelings— in a vain attempt to acquire a control they can never have—control of external events. The result is that they lose all control and suffer from even more stress in the bargain. The problem with this approach to stress management is, of course, that it is aimed at where they think the power is rather than at where it really is.

If I become stressed because I have given a person or a situation the power to intimidate me, I will not find the solution to my stress problem by manipulating that person or situation. I will eliminate my stress only when I begin working on the person who ought to have the power—me.

Mr. Long is a middle-aged engineering executive in a large corporation. He has been with the company for over twenty years, rising to his present post by internal promotion from the entry-level position he took right out of college. In a recent reorganization he was assigned an assistant, Dr. Young, a brilliant thirty-year-old with a Ph.D. from M.I.T. Mr. Long feels inadequate in his new assignment and inferior to his new assistant. He has become uptight, unfriendly and morose. He now spends much of his time trying to undermine Dr. Young's work and credibility.

Mr. Long has allowed his situation to intimidate him, and this has caused him to feel stressed. But all his efforts to manipulate the situation will not eliminate the stress because the stress did not originate with the company reorganization or with Dr. Young. It began when Mr. Long gave the situation the power to control him. Then, feeling out of control, he initiated a stress response to restore stability. Since his situation did not call for a physical response, all his stress was unnecessary and unpleasant. To eliminate his discomfort, Mr. Long tried to manipulate the situation to regain control. But he had no power over the situation. The only power available to him was the power to control his own feelings—and he had given that away. Until he recovers the power he gave away, he will remain completely powerless to deal with his stress.

All he has to do to regain that power is to claim it. He gave it away—he can take it back. With the recovery of his power, he can be back in control any time he wants to be. When he is in control, his life will be stable and he will not need a stress response. Very simply, this is the key to preventing excess stress: *Retain your own power, and use it constructively to establish and maintain emotional stability.*

As I said at the beginning of this chapter, it is important to clearly identify the origins of unwanted stress before attempting to eliminate the stress. If we mistakenly blame our stress on someone or something that did not cause it, we will probably use ineffective and damaging stress-motivated behaviors to try to get rid of it. If, on the other hand, we understand where stress comes from, we will reap two beneficial results. First, we will improve our ability to deal constructively with other people when their behavior is motivated by their unwanted stress. Second, we will be able to assess our own stress reactions and take the first steps toward stress prevention.

How to Suffer from Stress

1. Give to a person or situation the power to control how you feel about yourself.

2. Interpret that loss of control as a threat to your emotional stability (personal identity), so that your body will react to the instability with an unwanted stress response.

How to Amplify the Stress and Promote Conflict

1. Blame the source stimulus (person or situation) for your loss of control and your unwanted stress.

2. Try to manipulate the source to recover the power—any way you can.

3. Press the issue if you don't get immediate relief. Demand that the source change—now!

How to Recover Control

1. Recognize that you are (or can be) in charge of who you are.

2. Accept the reality of external things you cannot change.

3. Reclaim the power to decide who you are and stop sharing that power with the world.

Figure 7. Managing Personal Power

5 Foundations for a Stress-Free Life

BECAUSE I AM COMMITTED TO PREVENTION AS THE ONLY approach to stress management with any long-term value, I am frequently challenged by people who think it is too idealistic. "It all sounds very compelling," they say, "but it isn't practical. You can't expect people to be able just to stop feeling stressed. Life doesn't work that way."

Certainly I don't expect people to be able to prevent stress so long as they remain captive to the belief that the process is not theirs to control. But I believe without reservation that the process is subject to personal control and that every individual can, through faith, commitment and practice, learn to react to life in ways that do not provoke excess stress. Clearly the greatest obstacle to achieving this goal is the common belief that it cannot be accomplished.

Yet although I believe that anyone can rid his or her life of unwanted stress, I am not saying that this goal can be achieved without some cost. Stress prevention is possible—it is not necessarily easy. It is my purpose to show you how it can be done, to convince you that the cost is small when measured against the benefits derived from a life free from unwanted stress, and to help you develop the skills needed to make stress prevention a part of your daily life.

Ineffective Coping
The term *coping* is often used in association with efforts to control stress. As the term is usually used, coping is directed toward a situation that presents problems. It typically includes any action aimed at reducing personal stress. According to this understanding, those who cannot cope have stress, whereas those who can cope do not have stress. But as we have seen from our discussion of stress-motivated behavior, not all such action is effective or constructive.

For example, Mr. Nash had the habit of grinding his teeth. Mrs. Nash found this extremely irritating. In fact, after he retired and spent more time around the house, she could not seem to escape his long-playing molar music. She felt stressed almost constantly. Finally, unable to stand it any longer, she moved out and ultimately divorced him. Separation was Mrs. Nash's coping method. It eliminated what she perceived as the source of her stress, and, as she frequently acknowledged, it was more acceptable than strangling him, the only other coping method she had seriously considered.

At first glance, one might conclude that Mrs. Nash coped with her situation effectively. The divorce accomplished her primary goal—relieving her problem with stress. But let's look at the long-term result of Mrs. Nash's coping technique. Living alone after almost forty years with the same man, she felt lonely and unsure of herself. This unfamiliar situation caused her almost constant stress. Unable to endure it, she began to look for a new husband.

Through a singles group she met Mr. Grate, a man who reminded her in many ways of her former husband. After a brief courtship, they married.

Again, one might say that the new Mrs. Grate coped effectively. Her coping method, remarriage, eliminated the apparent source of her stress. But is her life now free of stress? Not at all. Mr. Grate has acquired the habit of grinding his teeth, and his wife, under perpetual stress because of it, is once again contemplating homicide. Is Mrs. Nash-Grate just terribly unlucky to have married two men who were both teeth-grinders? Of course not. These two men of similar personality used the same coping method, grinding their teeth, to deal with their own stress problem—living with a controlling spouse.

What did Mrs. Nash-Grate accomplish with her coping? Nothing—because coping, as she employed it and as people typically use it, never gets to the real source of stress. People get divorces, withdraw from society, take drugs and commit violence, all in the name of coping. But this kind of coping is nothing but a form of manipulation—a kind of game. As I have said before, making changes in life may be good and appropriate—but never as a method of manipulation to relieve stress.

This kind of coping may eliminate what you interpret to be the source of your stress, and it may give you temporary relief from the unpleasantness you experience in reaction to that source, but it does nothing to deal with the real origins of the stress. In fact, you can always tell when you have successfully dealt with your stress at its real point of origin. When you have done so, a situation which has always provoked you to stress in the past will no longer cause this reaction.

Mrs. Nash-Grate's coping technique did not deal with her real stress problem. If it had done so, her second husband's habit would not have provoked her exactly as her first husband's did. Blaming her husbands for her stress and dealing with them on that basis was a simple solution to her problem, but it was wrong. In the end, it was destructive. Mrs. Nash-Grate alone is responsible for her stress. Until she is willing to acknowledge this fact, she has no hope of constructively managing her stress problem.

If we want to manage stress effectively and permanently, our first goal cannot be to learn how to handle situations. It must instead be to learn how to prevent unwanted stress when such situations occur. The two approaches are completely different, and an understanding of this difference is fundamental to any effort to prevent unwanted stress. Again, I am not suggesting that it is wrong or unnecessary to manage situations. But managing situations is not related to preventing stress. Most people find, in fact, that they can manage situations much more effectively *after* they have learned how to prevent their unwanted stress.

Constructive stress management is a process consisting of a series of identifiable steps which need to be followed in sequence if the process is to work. The success of the process as a whole depends on how well each step is mastered as it is carried out. In this respect, stress management is like any other learning process. For example, the first step in learning to swim is overcoming one's fear of the water. If students are made to float, kick, stroke or dive before accomplishing the first step, failure is virtually assured. Their unconquered fear of the water will continually stand in the way of progress.

The Stress-Prevention Process
Before looking at the steps in stress prevention, we need to understand several attributes of the process. First, stress prevention is a specific application of the more general process I call life management. There are three stages in life management: appraising one's circumstances and personal capabilities (I can), appraising one's goal in relation to the probable cost (I want to), and declaring a personal commitment (I will). Each stage is mastered only when the

individual is able to say about it, truthfully and wholeheartedly,

I can!

I want to!

I will!

For example, on the first day of my weight-management classes, many participants want to jump right into stage three. They come in the door saying, "I will lose fifty pounds!" Yet the very reason they need help with their weight problem is that they have been trying to shortcut the three-stage process. They have never assessed the amount of sacrifice and commitment their goal will require, and they have never asked themselves if they are willing and able to pay the price. Like weight control, stress prevention follows the general sequence of the life-management process. It requires that each stage be accomplished before proceeding to the next.

Second, the stress-prevention process is totally subject to personal control. It can be successfully completed without any outside input. In fact, any attempt to abandon personal responsibility for the process will doom it to failure. Look again at the three statements that mark the completion of each stage of the life-management process. Each begins with the pronoun *I*. When I declare "I can," I am stating a personal decision. Only I can make this decision, and its outcome influences me alone. This attribute of the process is summarized in Ecker's Sixth Law: *Stress prevention is carried out in the first person singular.*

As I often tell my classes, "*I* am responsible for my own stress, and only *I* can do anything about it." In thus emphasizing personal choice and accountability, I am not leaving God out of the process. God created human beings with free will, the ability to choose the direction of their lives. Even though the effects of the Fall keep us from consistently making right choices on our own power, God still offers us the privilege of drawing on divine power as we manage our lives. He does not compel us to use his help; we are free to reject it. But whether I accept it or refuse it, the outcome—the direction of my life—depends on my personal choice. I am responsible for my own stress, and I am always in a position to do something about it. God will lend his strength to support me where I am weak, but I must choose to reach out and accept his strength. The choice is mine.

Third, the stress-prevention process is usually a lifelong undertaking. Most people who begin the process make some progress almost immediately. This is encouraging, but it is not enough. Once you begin to deal directly with the most troublesome causes of unwanted stress in your life, you will need time and perseverance to accomplish the goal of total stress prevention. As you use the process, you will gain insights into the nature of your problem. You will also discover tools for dealing with it and will learn how to put the tools to work.

I Can!

The first four steps in the stress-management process lead to awareness. Individuals who have completed these steps will know what stress is and who is responsible for it. They will understand the nature of the persons or situations that tend to provoke a stress response, and they will be in touch with their own identity. These four steps provide a basis of understanding that gives direction to the stress-management process.

Step 1—Understand what stress is. Clearly, it is hard to prevent stress if we do not understand what it is. As I have indicated before, stress is a physical response that the human body invokes in order to deal with a perceived threat to its stability. Stress is not a force in the external world; it is a response in the body. It becomes a problem only when the amount of stress produced exceeds the body's immediate need to deal physically with the threat. Stress is a necessary survival mechanism; only excess stress needs to be prevented.

Step 2—Accept the responsibility for your own stress. When I perceive that some source in the world is threatening my stability, I call on my stress response. How I perceive a source, however, is a matter of personal choice. I can choose to perceive it as a threat and react to it with a lot of stress, or I can choose to perceive it as neutral and react with no stress at all. Whatever my reaction, it comes from my conscious decision, and I alone am responsible for it. No matter how provocative a source is, it is never responsible for my stress—I am. And only when I have clearly understood and accepted my accountability can I hope to succeed in preventing stress.

The primary obstacle to taking the first two steps of the process is inertia. We have conditioned ourselves to believe that stress is "out there" and that we are not responsible for it. Now we find that, before we can deal with our stress, we must turn our thinking around. We have to be convinced that stress is "in here" and that we ourselves are totally responsible for it. That's a big change, and for some people it requires great effort. As an incentive to making that effort, remind yourself that the old way of thinking generates the life-management declaration, "I cannot." You are powerless to do anything about stress that is not yours to control. Taking responsibility for your stress re-establishes your authority over it and generates the life-management declaration, "I can!" But before you will be ready to make the second life-management declaration— "I want to!"—you need to come to terms both with the external situations that provoke stress in you and with your own personal identity. If you neglect steps 3 and 4, you may discover that you do not really want what you thought was important to you.

For example, when he started college, Ted said, "I want to be a surgeon." But he soon found out that he couldn't stand the sight of blood, was nauseated by formaldehyde and hated anatomy. The price to accomplish his "I want to!" was too high for Ted. Once he knew all the facts, he discovered he didn't want to be a surgeon after all. In fact, as he went to his adviser's office for a curriculum change form, he was overheard to say, "I want to be a newspaper reporter."

To say "I want to!" and mean it requires much careful consideration. For example, if I want to prevent an interpretive stress response, I have to identify and correct the error in my perception that initiates the response. Here are a few of the questions I may have to answer:

What is the real nature of the source?

How do I define stability in my life?

What aspect of that stability is threatened by the source?

To perceive the source correctly, what changes will I have to make?

How can I implement these changes?

From this brief list of questions, you can see how much is required just to find out if you truly want to deal with your stress. Honest answers to these questions can put you on the road toward understanding reality accurately and using that understanding as the basis for change. Steps 3 and 4 involve the search for reality.

Step 3—Find out the real identity of the source. Remember that the source does not cause stress. It is merely the place certain information came from. Unwanted stress occurs when we misread the information and therefore misidentify the source.

For example, when Mr. Popp, the boss, lost control and had a counterproductive stress response in reaction to his employee's low productivity, he was misreading reality. He obviously saw the employee, Mr. Fish, as a threat, or he would not have had a stress response. But was Mr. Fish an immediate threat to Mr. Popp's physical well-being? Of course not. We have to conclude that the boss's perception was mistaken.

What was the reality of the situation? The only pertinent reality was that Mr. Fish was undependable and unproductive. This reality certainly called for no physical response to protect the boss. Why, then, did Mr. Popp feel threatened? What caused him to respond to the situation with unnecessary and unwanted stress? He perceived a threat, and he confused that perception with reality. His only hope for a solution to his stress lies in his willingness to discover Mr. Fish's real identity. He has to accept this reality before he can deal with his own tendency to distort it.

Accepting a reality does not in any way require approval of it. It merely acknowledges the fact that the reality does not call for a stress response. Once Mr. Popp accepts the fact that Mr. Fish is lazy and irresponsible, he may decide to fire Mr. Fish or cut his pay or discipline him in some other way. He will not, however, develop headaches and high blood pressure and ruin his own afternoons, and he will not engage in stress-motivated attempts to get Mr. Fish to change his behavior, because he will understand that his physical response to Mr. Popp's workstyle is totally unnecessary.

From the standpoint of stress prevention, the most fundamental aspect of reality is identified in Ecker's Seventh Law: *It is impossible to control the events of life.* Just as a person in a watchtower cannot dictate the wind's velocity, so we have no real control over what happens in life. No one has the power to guarantee that everything will be exactly as desired. Those who think they have that power are among the most highly stressed people anywhere. Believing they can control events and having built their stability structures on that belief, they are constantly frustrated by human frailties (in others, not in themselves), acts of God and just plain bad luck. Predictably, such people find it impossible to avoid stress, and they will never be able to prevent it if they cling to the fantasy that they can control everything that may influence their emotional stability. But although we cannot control life events, we can, whenever we choose, maintain control over our feelings and our personal identities.

Who Am I?

Step 4—Get in touch with your own identity. In our initial discussion of interpretive stress responses, I defined the stability structure as the set of guiding principles we use to ensure emotional stability when our lives are subjected to uncertainty or threatened loss of control. The stability structure is essentially an interpreter through which we process all information coming to us from the world and assess how it influences us personally. If I have a stress response in circumstances that call for no such response, it is because my stability structure is not giving me an accurate interpretation. Since uncertainty is an inevitable part of life, the only way to have a life without unwanted stress is to overhaul my stability structure so that it gives me sound interpretations.

This overhauling is not an impersonal or mechanical operation. My stability structure is based in my self-concept. It gives me my identity. Thus changing my perception of reality necessarily involves changing my view of myself. A man who attended one of my workshops described the frustrations he faced in dealing with a teen-aged son who had behavioral problems. Tom disapproved of his son's attitudes and activities, and he constantly asked, "When is the boy going to find out who he is?" He found no answers, made no progress in his relationship with his son, and suffered increasing stress until he changed his question to, "When am *I* going to find out who he is?" The father didn't realize that there was an even more fundamental question he needed to face: "When am *I* going to find out who *I* am?" Finding the answer to that question is what step 4 is all about.

Step 4 is based on a proposition that is simple but difficult for many people to accept. We can call it Ecker's Eighth Law: *If you have a problem with unwanted stress, you have a problem with your self-concept.*

Interestingly, I find that people who seem to have particularly "high-stress" personalities usually protest my Eighth Law with great vigor. They typically believe that their self-image is good and that their stress is not of their own making. They defend their shaky stability structures and curse the forces in the world that they hold responsible for their stress. They would rather remain powerless in the face of unwelcome stress than acknowledge the need for personal change. But they will find no relief from their unwanted stress until they begin to investigate why their stability structures are so fragile.

"Who am I?" is a very important question. The answer will not be found in the world of fact—height, nose shape, eye color, age, marital status—but in the world of opinion. The *I* that holds the stability structure together is *who I think I am*. My self-concept is a personal belief that can be based on almost anything. To get in touch with the identity that is at the heart of my stability structure, I have to find out what the "almost anything" is in my life. What guiding principles mold my attitude of self-worth? Are they relevant to my present life? Do I want to keep them? Abandon them? Change them? Why?

Inspecting My Stability Structure
Carefully inspecting my stability structure will help me learn where its weak points are and determine what needs to be done to strengthen it. Since most of us are not accustomed to conducting such inspections, a few guidelines may be helpful. To begin, I need to review my stress reactions. What causes unwanted stress in my life? Whatever it is, it must be assaulting a vulnerable area in my structure, or I wouldn't be reacting with stress. Why is that situation or that person causing me to react with stress when none is required? An honest answer will tell me volumes about my stability structure.

Mrs. Trim, who spanked her adventurous and tattered four-year-old son, Jeff, had a stress response. She didn't need it, and she later regretted what it caused her to do. Then why did she have it? Her small son's behavior obviously hit something sensitive in her stability structure. He violated something in the set of guiding principles Mrs. Trim used to hold her life together. As a consequence, she felt personally violated, as if she were less of a person, because of her son's behavior. Her self-image had been attacked, even though the cause was only a four-year-old who was behaving like a four-year-old.

If Mrs. Trim inspected her stability structure, she would find it contains a group of elements we can call *conditions*. These elements set the conditions for establishing her value as a person. If life events permit the conditions to be met, her self-image receives positive support. But if events fail to satisfy her conditions, her self-worth decreases. Mrs. Trim's stability structure may contain a condition requiring her offspring to behave in an exemplary manner. If he does so, her self-worth remains intact. If he does not, her self-worth suffers. She may also find a condition requiring her life to be free of unnecessary work and aggravation. If she has to run an extra load of wash and mop the kitchen floor a second time, her self-worth decreases.

By establishing and maintaining this conditional identity, Mrs. Trim has given the events of life the power to determine her self-worth. If she wants to live her life without unwanted stress, these identity conditions will have to go. Yet, identifying and removing conditions will not be a one-time job for Mrs. Trim. Every time she faces a stress situation, she will have to follow the same inspection process, to pinpoint the real origins of her stress and to show her what changes will be necessary to strengthen her stability structure.

When is the best time to inspect the stability structure? Remember the watchtower in the windy locale. If you inspect the base of the tower on a calm day, you are not likely to find the tower's weak areas. The time to find the places that need reinforcing is when the wind is blowing. So when you want to know where to strengthen your stability structure, look at it when it's being assaulted—when you are under stress.

Some years ago, when my eldest daughter was a teen-ager, she disobeyed me openly and defiantly in front of some of her friends, all of whom I viewed with suspicion and disapproval. I had a stress response—a violent one—and I beat the child mercilessly in front of her friends. I had always been a highly self-assured individual and would have argued vehemently against any suggestion that my self-image had problems. But the stark violence of my reaction shook me so that I took a closer look at myself. Why did I find it necessary to respond with such an overwhelming physical reaction when my only assailant was a skinny little fifteen-year-old girl? The answer was obvious—I had interpreted my daughter's actions as a violation of my self-worth. It was equally obvious that, if I hoped to live the rest of my life with some degree of freedom from stress, I would have to begin looking at the conditions I had been using to structure my self-image.

I take no pride in confessing that it required such an act of violence for me to ask that all-important question, "Why?" I sincerely hope that others can be motivated to ask it without driving themselves to such extremes. But I thank God I was forced to do so, because otherwise I would have found no answer. And without the answer, I could never have begun to deal with my own stress or to relate honestly and lovingly to my daughter.

The purpose of step 4 in the stress-prevention process is to confirm the need for personal change and to identify the areas in which change is required. Once you have a firm understanding of reality, of your own stability structure, and of the nature of stress, you are able to say, "I can!" Now you can decide whether you are ready to progress to the next declaration—"I want to!"

6 Making the Change

*A*RE YOU WILLING TO PAY THE PRICE REQUIRED TO eliminate your stress? Ecker's Ninth Law says: *The price of stress prevention is personal change.*

Personal change is not easy. Most of us have invested a lot of emotional energy in the standards and principles that give us our identity. If these standards and principles fail to insulate us from stress, we would rather claim that our stability structure is not involved than think about changing it. We would rather sit in our shaking towers and curse the wind than risk finding weaknesses in the support structures. This common human tendency is reflected in Ecker's Tenth Law: *The greater your problem with stress, the more unwilling you will be to admit your need for change and the more difficulty you will have implementing the change.*

The Tenth Law is an optimistic restatement of the dogmatic

axiom of a clinician I know. He states categorically, "Controllers never change." People who have a strong need for control invest a great deal of energy in constructing what they hope will be a protective stability structure. Controllers can and do change, but it can be especially hard for them to see the limitations in their stability structure and to abandon its destructive elements. But no one can make progress in dealing with personal stress unless he or she is willing to change. The stress-prevention process grinds to a halt until the individual can say with conviction, "I want to!" This fifth step in stress prevention recognizes the need for change and honestly evaluates what these changes will require in terms of personal sacrifice.

Step 5—Count the cost. When you say you want to continue the stress-management process, you are declaring your willingness to risk whatever investment you have in your present identity in order to acquire a new identity that cannot be threatened. Mary Ann finds such a declaration extremely difficult to make. A highly educated, highly intelligent woman, she has a passion for accuracy and a powerful need to be right. When her viewpoint is challenged, she becomes tense, irritable and loudly argumentative. If she is accused of making a mistake, she will stew for hours, trying to justify herself or pass on the blame to someone else. Such episodes always give her headaches.

Mary Ann has a big investment in being right. Perfection is the standard she sets for herself, and she will accept nothing less. It is, in fact, the condition she depends on for confirming her self-worth. When this condition is challenged by evidence of imperfection, her stability structure is shaken and she reacts with stress. Before Mary Ann can hope to deal with this stress, she must accept the fact that her self-concept is faulty. She will have to abandon those conditions which, for many years, have been the prime elements of her self-image. If she finds that price too high, then she will be wasting her time trying to prevent stress.

Stress Doesn't Help

It may be easier for Mary Ann to abandon her stress-producing perfectionism if she considers Ecker's Eleventh Law: *Stress will not alter the outcome.*

Of all the stress-prevention principles, this is the one most people find hardest to acknowledge and put into practice. Yet because the principle is pivotal to the stress-prevention process, it must become part of our stability structure before we can be fully equipped to conquer unwanted stress.

Imagine that a close loved one has been seriously injured in a traffic accident. You have been called to the emergency room in the middle of the night, and for an hour you have been sitting on an uncomfortable bench waiting for word of your loved one's condition. The reality of your situation is obvious—someone you care for is in danger. What is an appropriate response to that reality?

Most people respond with stress. Their pulses race; their nerves are on edge; they pace the floor to deal with the energy reserves their bodies have called up to meet the crisis. But can your stress response alter the outcome? Can it restore damaged organs, give skill to the physicians or even communicate your caring to the patient? Not in the slightest. You have no power over the situation, and the most intense stress reaction on your part is not going to enable you to change it.

No one ever wants to be powerless. So we all tend to deny reality and try to change it with our stress reactions. Like a golfer moving his arms and shoulders to urge an errant ball toward the cup or a passenger pressing his right foot against the car floor to prevent a head-on collision, we use "body English" to try to get our way in impossible situations. We hope our physical reactions will influence something that is completely beyond our control. The result, inevitably, is excess stress and frustration.

Dr. Robert Eliot, a cardiologist and authority on the role of stress in heart disease, gave a highly competitive business executive an impossible task and then observed his physiological signs of excess stress. When these signs approached the danger point, Dr. Eliot told the executive to stop. The man protested, saying he could master the task with just a little more time. Dr. Eliot responded, "Is it worth dying for?" (*American Medical News*, 15 May 1981). The business executive thought that even more stress could alter the outcome, but Dr. Eliot knew it could not. The physician's question is a good one to consider when we feel our own stress level rising.

When we find ourselves unable to alter the outcome of situations that are important to us, we often assume that we are supposed to have a stress reaction—and so we do. At these times we are not guided by what is appropriate and helpful, but rather by what we think society expects of us. If a loved one is in intensive care, for example, we feel compelled to have a physical reaction so that others will not label us "unfeeling." This association of stress with caring is completely fallacious. Ecker's Twelfth Law says: *You don't need stress to care.*

Concern is not a stress reaction and does not require stress in order to be honest and meaningful. Truly concerned people do what they can to help those they care for, but stress is more likely to hurt than to help.

In our fast-paced society, we have become so accustomed to excess stress that we seem unable to think of living without it. Our attitude is neatly expressed by the motto: "If you can remain calm while everyone around you is going crazy . . . you obviously don't understand the situation."

Although the motto is meant to be humorous, it represents a common attitude. Excess stress is so common that we think there is something wrong with someone who doesn't have any. Some participants in my stress-management workshops have protested that without excess stress they would become so "laid back," so unfeeling, that they would be nothing but robots. Sales managers have worried that an unstressed salesperson would be next to useless. Others have suggested that air-traffic controllers would be unable to do their job properly without being under constant stress. This point of view is completely wrong.

As Ecker's Twelfth Law points out, you don't need excess stress in order to express normal, healthy feelings. You don't need it in order to remain alert and attentive to detail. Stress is not the same as concern. It is a physical response to prepare a person for extraordinary physical action. When you actually need the stress response, it will be there.

Think about the last time you were startled by an unexpected loud noise. How long did it take you to respond with a typical stress reaction? Did it take several minutes and a great deal of effort for you to jump, to feel your heart thumping or the hair at the back of your neck bristling? No, it took only a fraction of a second. That's all the time it takes for stress to come to your aid when you need it.

So if you can call on your stress response at any time and have it serve you immediately, what is the value of remaining constantly stressed in anticipation of a possible need? Being under constant excess stress doesn't make an individual more "feeling" in relations with others; it doesn't give the salesperson a more aggressive personality; and it doesn't make the air-traffic controller better able to do the job. In fact, in the long run, it works against every one of these results. Stress prevention will take nothing away from you that your life would not be better without.

The Commitment to Change

Do the benefits of stress prevention sound good enough to go after? Do you really want to rid your life of excess stress, even though you will have to make major changes in your stability structure—your identity—to do so? If you do, then take a look at the kind of commitment such changes will involve—what it will require to say "I will" and really mean it.

Step 6—Commit to change. Anyone who has ever tried to implement a major change—to quit smoking or to lose twenty pounds, for example—knows that even a firm commitment to the task doesn't guarantee it will be easy. And eliminating your stress will not be easy. But any task is easier to deal with when we understand what is involved and when we have guidelines for accomplishing it.

We're talking here about a specific kind of personal change—a change in self-image. The first thing we have to understand is that we are not dealing with fact but with viewpoint; we are not talking about *what is* but about *what we believe.* Understanding this will give you the one tool you need to proceed—control of the process. You are in charge of what you believe. Your belief system is yours to do with as you please.

Your self-image is your estimate of your value as a human being. But what gives you value? Is your life more valuable because you can play the piano or solve complex mathematical problems? Is it more valuable because you teach Sunday school or spend every Thursday as a hospital volunteer? Is it more valuable because people think you are good looking or have a pleasant personality?

If any of these are true, then is your life less valuable because you can't play the piano as well as your sister or don't understand Einstein? Is it less valuable if you go to Sunday school unprepared or miss a Thursday at the hospital? Is it less valuable because some people do not consider you particularly good looking and others think you're a bore?

The problem is that for every "I can," you can find an "I can't"; for every "I do," an "I don't"; for every "I am," an "I'm not." However favorable the overall public opinion of you, someone out there will find some flaws in you. Only when you accept your personal worth as an intrinsic value—an indisputable fact—will it be secure and unshakable. Why? Because your intrinsic identity exists only in your belief system. Your merit as a human being is what you believe it to be, and only you can alter that belief. Your abilities, your activities, your physical features and what others think of you are matters of fact. Your self-image is a matter of faith.

So when your self-image has flaws, these flaws are strictly self-imposed. They exist because you have placed conditions on your identity. You have qualified your self-image with "ifs" and "whens"—"I am somebody *if* . . ." or "I am somebody *when* . . ." Whenever you fail to measure up to your conditions, your self-worth diminishes. And as long as you continue to harbor these conditions in your identity structure, your self-image will be subject to destruction by the events of life. Self-imposed conditions lead to a poor self-image and unwanted stress.

Mary Ann, the perfectionist, bases her self-concept on two conditions—what she can do and how others evaluate what she can do. She is very good at what she does, but not so good that she never makes mistakes. She is an accomplished person, but others still find flaws in her from time to time. As long as she bases her self-image on these conditions, it is doomed to instability—she is destined to a life of frequent unwanted stress.

To change all that, all she has to do is to change what she believes—to eliminate the conditions. She can choose to believe that her value as a human being is not based on what she can do or how others view her, but on her creation in the image of God. She can opt to accept her own intrinsic worth as a matter of faith. If she makes this choice and begins to believe, "I am somebody special"—with no "ifs" or "whens"—on what authority can anybody dispute her conclusions? It's Mary Ann's self-image. She can make it anything she wants it to be. And if she wants it to be independent of external events, she will eliminate her conditions, the primary cause of her unwanted stress.

Similarly, the harried housewife who bases her identity on the cleanliness of her kitchen, the uptight salesman who bases his self-worth on being liked by others, the frustrated ex-athlete whose self-image is grounded in past glories—all can choose to eliminate their conditions and reinvest themselves in an identity that, by faith, declares unequivocally, "I am somebody special." When they make that declaration of faith, they prohibit events from influencing their emotional stability and neutralize the need for unwanted stress.

It should be apparent, then, that successful stress prevention has one fundamental requirement—to purge my identity of self-destructive conditions. As long as I allow events to dictate my concept of personal worth, as long as I qualify my self-image with "ifs" and "whens," I will continue to respond with stress when situations don't satisfy my conditions. If, on the other hand, I exercise my prerogative as the author of my self-image and remove the conditions from my identity structure, external events will have no influence on my identity. Thus these events will not be able to elicit unwanted stress.

Unfortunately, most people find it a lot easier to accept this solution in principle than to put it into practice. Personal change is never easy, particularly when we have a big investment in the way things are. But those of us who who base our personal belief systems on the Word of God have a way of simplifying the solution immeasurably.

The biggest problem a person faces in amending his or her identity structure is establishing a credible basis of authority for the new one. Who gives anyone the right to say that he or she is a person of intrinsic value? Christians have an answer—God gives each one of us that right. The Bible teaches that God created us in his image and redeemed us through the gift of his Son. Our salvation—our worth in God's eyes—is not a matter of personal accomplishment, but is a matter of divine grace. People who submit to God's authority have the universe's best authority for declaring that they are valuable human beings. Their commitment to change is based not on shallow hope, but on unwavering assurance.

7 The Image of God

A PERSON'S SELF-IMAGE IS A PRODUCT OF HIS OR HER belief system. It is a matter of faith rather than of fact. Christianity provides a strong authority for a healthy self-image; other religions offer a less secure foundation. But whether a person is overtly religious or not, everyone has a belief system. Everyone accepts certain ideas and values as matters of faith, and all such matters of faith have some sort of higher authority behind them. The authority may not be a deity, and faith in the authority may not be expressed in religious practice, but authority is necessary to any belief system.

Secular humanists, for example, find their authority in man. They believe that man is the center of all that is important. Achieving man's aspirations and solving man's problems are their primary goals, and they judge everything according to how well it helps them do this. Secular humanists base their self-image on a human standard of their own creation. It can be weak or it can be strong, but it can never be stronger than they are themselves. It cannot help them grow.

Christians, on the other hand, find their authority in the Word of God. The Bible teaches that God created human beings in his own image. Its manifold promises show that the Creator places high value on his human creatures, in spite of their shortcomings. When Christians base their self-image on the authority of God's Word, they are taking a step of faith. They are believing they are what God says they are, even if they do not always feel that way. They can do this because God's Word is a trustworthy source of authority.

It is a common human tendency to establish identity on the basis of what one *does* or *can do* rather than on who one *is*. Ask a typical group of people to complete the statements, "I am somebody because . . ." or "I am nobody because . . . ," and the most frequent responses will relate to personal accomplishments or failures—what I have defined as identity conditions. How do such conditions fit what we know about human identity from the Word of God? They don't fit at all. In fact, identity based on accomplishment has no place at all in God's Word. Our only significant identity as Christians is based on being created in the image of God. And that identity is not acquired by personal accomplishment—it is a gift of God.

Created in His Image

In the Creation story, God planned and executed the formation of human beings "in his own image" (Gen 1:27). It may not be clear from Scripture how man came into his biological identity, but the Word leaves no doubt about how he acquired his self-image. All human beings are created bearing the mark of the Creator, an identity we are privileged to carry, if we choose, throughout all of our days. God gives us the simplest possible way to finish the statement, "I am somebody because . . ." As a consequence of my creation in his image, I can state unequivocally, "I am somebody because God made me somebody."

On a scale of one to ten, everything God makes is a ten. He is incapable of making anything less. The identity he hands us cannot be improved upon. How is it, then, that we so often end up carrying around such awful self-images? Very simply, it's because we grow discontented with the basis for the image God gave us. We begin to believe we can find, in our own merits, a more valid basis for personal identity. We put ourselves in the image-making business. But improving on God is just not possible—not with what we have to work with.

What do we have to work with? Very little if we hope to build an identity on personal merit. Paul gave an excellent inventory of our working materials when he declared, "I do not understand my own actions. For I do not do what I want, but I do the very thing I hate. . . . I know that nothing good dwells within me, that is, in my flesh. I can will what is right, but I cannot do it. For I do not do the good I want, but the evil I do not want is what I do" (Rom 7:15, 18-19). When we build our concept of personal value on what we can *do*, we find, like Paul, that we have nothing to work with but faulty materials. The resulting self-image is destined to be as faulty as the materials from which it is made. A person who measures his or her own achievements against God's standard is forced to admit, "I am nobody."

The stability structure always interprets life events from the perspective of the self-image. It evaluates events by the question, "How does this event influence my concept of self-worth?" When I base my self-image on personal merit, my stability structure often sees events as a challenge to my identity. When my identity is challenged, my emotions are thrown into instability and unwanted stress occurs. So in simple terms, unwanted stress occurs because people choose to second-guess the identity God has given them. They reject their identity as the image of God, which is part of their natural inheritance as his children, and they build an identity based on personal accomplishment instead. Fortunately, to solve the problem of unwanted stress is as simple to understand as the cause: *Get out of the image-making business.*

In dealing with unwanted stress, one of the most difficult truths to accept is the fact that stress prevention is not fundamentally a matter of behavior. It is a matter of faith. Ecker's Eighth Law points out that unwanted stress exists because of a self-image problem. A person whose concept of self-worth cannot be negatively influenced by life events will have no excess stress. How do we obtain such an unassailable self-image? We already have it. It is the image of God, given to us at our creation. All we are required to do is to accept the authority of God's Word and to use his image as the *sole* basis of our personal identity. It takes faith to do this—faith in God's power, his love, and his accessibility.

A Matter of Faith

Jesus spoke this difficult truth emphatically when he was teaching his disciples about dealing with stress. On many different occasions he addressed their anxieties with the same comment, "O men [man] of little faith" (Mt 6:30; 8:26; 14:31; 16:8; Lk 12:28). Their problem with stress was not a consequence of troublesome life events. It did not result from their inability to relax. It was simply a matter of too little faith. They were unwilling to accept at face value God's promises, as revealed not only by the prophets of old but also by his flesh-and-blood presence among them. They wanted to be Jesus' disciples, but they were not always prepared to trust him and obey him.

It is no different with us today. If Jesus were now walking the streets of our cities and towns, how would he react to our anxieties? If he questioned Peter's faith when he couldn't walk on water, how would he view our tendency to respond with stress in the slightest tribulation? Certainly his words would echo in our homes, our churches, our board rooms and our governmental assemblies—"Which of you by being anxious can add one cubit to his span of life? . . . Seek first his kingdom and his righteousness, and all these things shall be yours as well" (Mt 6:27, 33).

Yet in emphasizing the role of faith in attaining freedom from unwanted stress, God is not insensitive to the struggles we face in placing our trust totally in him. He knows we cannot even have faith on our own; "it is the gift of God," Paul says (Eph 2:8). So in his infinite love, God has put his own resources at our disposal to help us in the struggle. Consider, for example, the following assurances from his Word that his resources are continually available to us:

Cast your burden on the LORD, and he will sustain you. [Ps 55:22]

Trust in the LORD for ever, for the LORD GOD is an everlasting rock. [Is 26:4]

If you abide in me, and my words abide in you, ask whatever you will, and it shall be done for you. [Jn 15:7]

We know that in everything God works for good with those who love him, who are called according to his purpose. [Rom 8:28]

My grace is sufficient for you, for my power is made perfect in weakness. [2 Cor 12:9]

I can do all things in him who strengthens me. [Phil 4:13]

He has said, "I will never fail you nor forsake you." Hence we can confidently say, "The Lord is my helper, I will not be afraid; what can man do to me?" [Heb 13:5-6]

Our problem is not the availability of power to control the factors that cause unwanted stress. It is in making the personal commitment that is required before we can share in that power. This commitment is *faith*. In essence, we are involved in a struggle between our self-made conditions and God's unconditional assurance.

I have been an active, vocally confessing Christian for most of my adult life. I have always been deeply involved in the activities of my local congregation and in the work of the church at large. I have consistently claimed to believe every one of those scriptural promises of God's helping power. Yet when the stark violence of my actions against my daughter forced me to ask, "Why?" I had to inspect my own stability structure and assess the real authority behind my self-image.

The inspection revealed that my claims of faith were nothing but lip service. I was carrying around a self-image that completely rejected my identity as a child of God and substituted an identity conditional on personal authority. Any assault on that authority violated my identity and diminished my sense of self-worth. I could not say "I am somebody" unless my rules were obeyed. If they were disobeyed, I had to say "I am nobody," because the challenge to my authority disrupted my identity structure. As my identity structure crumbled, I invoked a violent stress response.

Once I discovered the conditions I had been using to maintain my sense of personal worth, I could seek a better way. I found this better way in the beliefs I had been neglecting in spite of my confessions of faith. In God's promises I found forgiveness for my shortcomings and hope for a positive, unconditional personal identity. These promises assure me that, without any action or merit on my part, I am somebody special. I was created to be a living, breathing image of God.

What do you have to do to be somebody special? Only believe. Believe in God's promises; believe in the unquestionable authority behind your right to claim his image. There is no more inspiring example of such faith than that of the patriarch Abraham as described by Paul in his letter to the Romans. Recounting Abraham's response to God's unbelievable promise that he would be the father of a great nation, Paul writes, "No distrust made him waver concerning the promise of God, but he grew strong in his faith as he gave glory to God, fully convinced that God was able to do what he had promised" (Rom 4:20-21).

Yet Abraham was not always the bastion of faith that Paul describes here. Earlier he was our example of distrust in God, as evidenced by his stress-motivated attempt to pass off Sarah as his sister to protect his own skin. Nonetheless, with God's help he overcame his distrust and grew in faith. His faith became so strong that he was willing to sacrifice his only son in obedience to God's command; it became so assured that he could confidently declare to Isaac, "God will provide himself the lamb for a burnt offering, my son" (Gen 22:8).

Like Abraham, we can overcome our dependence on conditions and experience the growth in faith that leads to complete trust in God's unconditional grace. We too can give glory to God, fully assured that he is able to do all that he has promised.

8 Stress and Marriage

*M*OST PEOPLE FIND THAT THEIR GREATEST PROBLEMS with stress arise from their relations with other people. Any setting which puts people in regular contact with one another has significant potential for stress. And when people's lives are closely interdependent—when the activities of one affect the lives of the others—the potential for stress increases. The greater the investment in the relationship, the greater the likelihood of stress and conflict. Obviously, the family heads the list of potentially stressful settings, and the workplace is a close second.

Emotionally motivated stress typically occurs in response to a perceived loss of control over one's circumstances. Clearly, when a relationship requires sharing control with another person—spouse, parent, child, friend, supervisor, employee, colleague—the possibility for conflict is greater than when no such sharing occurs. We need to understand the concept of shared control if we want to put

our stress-analysis skills to work on improving personal relationships. *Shared control occurs whenever one person's activities have
a significant influence on the life events of another person—*
whenever one person loses some or all control of his or her own life
because of dependence on the actions of another person.

For example, Mr. Crock is an alcoholic. He lives with his wife and
two school-aged children. In the past year he has had three jobs,
and his present one is in jeopardy because of his drinking. Although
Mrs. Crock has taken a job to help cover expenses, she never knows
if her husband will contribute his share to the family budget or wipe
out both their paychecks with a credit spending spree. Twice in the
last month Mr. Crock has been brought home in a police car because
he couldn't make it on his own. The family is embarrassed by his
behavior and frustrated with the situation. Mrs. Crock is in an
almost perpetual state of stress. The children alternate between
hating their father for what he does to them and feeling guilty for
their lack of support.

The lives of these four people are closely linked. Virtually
anything one of them does affects the lives of the other three; that
is, it diminishes their control over their own circumstances. Most
of the current problems in the Crock family appear to result from
Mr. Crock's alcoholism. Mrs. Crock and the children feel powerless
because, although his condition affects their lives in many
important ways, it is entirely beyond their control. But their actions
also affect Mr. Crock's life. For example, if Mrs. Crock and the
children suddenly moved out, Mr. Crock would have no one to cook
for him, make excuses for him or pay the rent. His life would change
enormously within just a few days.

When, by choice or by chance, we become part of a relationship,
our lives are affected by many factors beyond our control. If we
perceive such loss of control as a threat to our stability, the frequent
result will be unwanted stress. As a consequence, our relationships
will probably be subject to frequent conflict. The current high rate

of divorce, the high incidence of drug abuse and suicide (particularly among teen-agers), and the frequent occurrence of family violence all indicate how poorly prepared we are to accept the sharing of personal control that characterizes meaningful interpersonal relationships.

Most of us choose to marry and to have children, but few of us realize the amount of personal control we will be required to give up as the result of those choices. I can recall standing watch over a croupy infant in a makeshift steam tent and saying to myself, "Just remember, you were born single." Some people, reacting with stress to this loss of control, attempt to regain control in order to eliminate the stress. When they do this, they take a big step toward destroying the relationship. In this chapter we will look at stress and control in the husband-wife relationship; in the next two chapters we will focus on two other important relationships—parent-child and employer-employee.

Clinging to Control

Earlier we met Mr. and Mrs. Ace, a couple who played World War 3 on the way home from a party. Married couples frequently play World War 3 as they attempt to control their individual stress responses. In this game, each player feels out of control and blames the other player for that fact. Each also feels that the only way to regain control is for the other to change. So they shout, point fingers and resurrect outdated sins, each trying to eliminate the unpleasantness of unwanted personal stress. The dynamics of World War 3 are simple: each time the husband makes a cutting remark to regain control for himself, the wife assumes that *he* has all the control. She redoubles her own efforts to get it back, thereby making the husband fear that *she* has all the control. The interaction quickly spirals into chaos. The game usually ends with one participant performing the ultimate manipulation—unilateral termination of the game and withdrawal, either through silence or by leaving the scene, often with a slammed door as a "last word."

World War 3 may seem mildly amusing as we describe it here, but for the participants it is deadly serious business. Interestingly, it happens almost exclusively with married people or others who have a close personal relationship. We would be very surprised to see such furious emotional combat carried on by two strangers. Why? Because strangers don't have any emotional investment in each other. They don't share life control.

Have you ever observed a married couple who have agreed to divorce, but are still living together until the details of the separation are worked out? It's not unusual to hear their friends describe the relationship as "living like strangers." They don't fight anymore. They are civil, but distant. Both have withdrawn their investment in the relationship. What the husband does is no longer viewed by the wife as a factor in her control of life events, and what the wife does no longer affects the husband. The basis of conflict has been removed.

If such a situation does not result in ending the conflict, it is clear that one or both of the parties have retained a significant investment in the relationship in spite of the agreement for separation and divorce. I don't want the subject of divorce to dominate our discussion on stress in the marriage relationship, but we have to recognize that it is currently the commonest solution to married people's inability to share control. It is also an excellent illustration of the consequences of making an investment in a relationship without accepting the loss of control that goes with it. Willingly sharing control of life is absolutely essential to maintaining healthy personal relationships.

As marriage partners strive to prevent stress in their relationship, each of them needs to become particularly attuned to the nature of the source (the other partner) and what each perceives that source to be. Step 3 of the stress-prevention process is the one that concerns us here—finding out the real identity of the source.

I once observed a game of World War 3 in which the conflict revolved around whether the cole slaw from a fast-food franchise was better than that made by one partner's mother. Can you imagine two strangers fighting over such an issue? The issue, of course, was not really cole slaw, but control. Cole slaw was only a prop in the game. The real problem was that neither partner had an accurate concept of reality; neither understood what the other was really like. For each, the true cause of stress was not the spouse, but a perception of lost control because of the spouse's actions and an unwillingness to give up that control.

Giving Up Control

To prevent stress-induced outbreaks of warfare in marital relationships, these realities must be accepted:

1. Successful marriage always involves a dilution of personal control because successful relationships are built on personal investment (that is, the transfer to someone else of control over an outcome that is important to you).

2. Once that investment has been made, control cannot be recovered without substantially redefining the relationship.

3. The identity of your marriage partner does not change when you make that investment. The only thing that changes is your own level of control. In making the investment, you choose to allow the other person's activities to influence (control) certain aspects of your life.

4. When your partner's activities threaten your emotional stability, the resulting unwanted stress will not be eliminated by a change in your partner's actions but by a change in your perspective on control. You have no assured control over your partner's actions, but you have complete control over how you react to them.

I am not saying that one partner will never change his or her behavior out of thoughtfulness for the other partner. Certainly you should ask your spouse to change his or her actions if you think such a change will make your life together more rewarding. Just remember that your partner's actions are not the cause of your stress, and that you can choose to eliminate your stress whether or not your partner ever changes. Take the case of Mrs. Crock and her alcoholic husband. She is constantly stressed in reaction to his behavior. Although she has tried desperately to get him to change, he has not. So she remains stressed—and will continue to be stressed for as long as she permits his activities to control her emotions. If she wants to get rid of her stress, she will have to reconsider the way she is allowing the dilution of control to affect her emotional stability.

To deal with her problem, Mrs. Crock needs to be reminded of Ecker's Eleventh and Twelfth Laws: *Stress will not alter the outcome,* and *You don't need stress to care.* Mr. Crock's alcoholism is a significant problem, but it won't change simply because Mrs. Crock experiences unnecessary, unwanted and unhealthy stress in reaction to it. And it is essential for Mrs. Crock to realize that she doesn't have to abandon concern for Mr. Crock just because she elects to stop feeling stressed over his problem. As in any other situation, stress in marriage relationships occurs by choice, not by chance. You can choose not to react to your partner with stress. It all depends on how you elect to perceive the situation.

Stress comes into a human relationship when one of the parties in the relationship is unwilling to share control with the other party or parties. Thus the only way to eliminate the stress is to learn how to share control—that is, to willingly make one's life dependent on others' activities. To accomplish this, we will need to know what loss of control is going to cost.

How do we count the cost of giving up control? It's very simple, really. We only need to figure out what we are trying to protect when we resist sharing control. And we already know what that is—our self-image. People crave control because they feel that in order to preserve their identities, they must maintain control over events in their lives. Thus when they share control, they feel they have given away the power to regulate their own self-worth.

For example, Mr. Tick feels that being on time is an essential part of his identity. He has a condition in his stability structure which states, "If I am late, I am less." Mrs. Tick, on the other hand, would not think of leaving the house without being impeccably dressed, made up, jeweled and coifed. She has a condition in her structure which states, "If I am not beautifully turned out, I am less." For her, being late is a small price to pay for looking good.

When the Ticks go somewhere together, something has to give. Usually they are late because, in this instance, Mrs. Tick controls the schedule. This causes Mr. Tick considerable stress and frequently strains the relationship. A part of Mr. Tick's life which he considers crucial to his identity is no longer under his control. He shares that control with his wife, and he doesn't like what she does with it. He thinks he is a hapless victim of her irresponsibility, and of course he blames her for the stress he experiences.

But, as you well know, she is not responsible for his stress. It occurs because he chooses to tie his identity to events and his own accomplishments. The only way he can eliminate his stress is to stop basing his self-image on his achievements. When he is able to do that, he will no longer be unwilling to share control with his wife. This doesn't mean that his wife is right in her way of dealing with life, or that they shouldn't discuss their differences and seek a solution; it merely acknowledges that her activities, even though they will affect his life, can never alter his identity.

In a healthy, stress-free relationship, the participants are all able to accept the realities of their situation. They understand that those realities, no matter who controls them, have no influence on personal identity. They accept the fact that true identity comes from the love of God and not from the acts of other human beings. And they know that no one but themselves can cause their identity to be less than God intended it to be.

9 Stress and Parenting

*L*IKE THE MARRIAGE RELATIONSHIP, THE PARENT-CHILD relationship involves a large emotional investment by both parties. And as in all interpersonal relationships, this investment causes a dilution of personal control: the actions of one party impose conditions on the life of the other. This loss of control has the potential to cause stress. However, in the parent-child relationship, stress and its consequences may result not only from the existence of mutual dependence, but also from the requirement that this dependence change as the child matures.

Because adolescence is the stage of child development that usually provokes the most stress in the parent-child relationship, I will concentrate my discussion on that period of development. But before turning to the specific concerns of parents of teen-agers, I want to look at one aspect of stress-motivated behavior among parents which is completely unrelated to the child's developmental stage. This behavior has become widespread in today's society, and its effects are potentially disastrous to the young people involved. One specialist in child development has labeled it *hurrying*.

The Hurrying Game

Hurrying is an effort on the part of a parent to accelerate a child's maturation process, to get the child to grow up faster. Although this parental behavior can affect almost any aspect of maturation, it is most commonly focused on the child's accomplishments in sports, the arts or scholarship. An excellent discussion of the effects of hurrying on the child's development is found in *The Hurried Child* by Dr. David Elkind (Reading, Mass.: Addison Wesley, 1981). I will limit my own comments to two areas: the role of stress in motivating this kind of parental action, and the effect of hurrying on the child's stress resistance.

Hurrying is a parental game. Like all games, it has an admirable declared purpose and a destructive ulterior motive. Parents who hurry their children argue that accelerated development is good for them. This is pure fantasy. Not only is hurrying not beneficial to the child, it upsets normal developmental progress by imposing unreasonable performance requirements and by confusing the child's concept of the world.

The real purpose of hurrying is not to benefit the child, but to eliminate parental stress. Parents who play this game are looking for reassurance that they are able to produce above-average offspring. The child is merely an object of manipulation—a pawn in a behavioral game. Like all such games, this one typically fails to accomplish its intended purpose. Parents who base their own hope for identity reinforcement on unreasonable expectations of their children are courting frequent disappointment. The hurrying game also plays havoc with the relationships among some or all the participants, and it causes both immediate and long-term problems for the child by interfering with the normal developmental process.

In their efforts to preserve their own stability, parents often fail to realize that they are the most important source of stability in their children's lives. The world is a scary place for a little child, and often even for a big one. As we grow into adulthood, we become used to things going wrong around us and we tend to forget what it was like to face the world with only a few years of life behind us. Recently, while cleaning up some accumulated junk in the garage, I came across a small brass bell. On an impulse, I hooked it to the collar of our little dog, Suzi, where it added its gentle tinkling to the jangle of the various metal name tags and immunization records she always carries around with her. Some time later my daughter asked, "What's wrong with the dog?"

Suzi sat trembling under my daughter's chair. She would hardly move, and, when she did, it was with the utmost caution, trying her best not to ring the bell. As soon as we removed the bell, she became her frisky self again. From my perspective, the little bell was a harmless toy. To the dog, it was a frightening mystery, full of uncertainty and possible danger. Like many parents who try to impose adult perspectives on their children, I expected the dog to perceive the bell as I did. But she was not capable of seeing it my way. Her experience was too limited. To her, the bell was a source of instability—and she reacted with stress.

Parents are the child's guardians of stability. By hurrying the child, they abdicate this role and leave the young person wondering whose side the parents are on. For the child, this can make an already scary world into a nightmare. Even so, the hurried child will usually strive for the grown-up goals in the parents' "game plan." After all, the pressuring parents are the only source of stability the child has known. But the ambiguities introduced by the parents' manipulations will greatly increase the likelihood of excess stress in the life of the child. This in turn will promote the dire developmental consequences that chronic stress can be expected to cause in an emotionally immature personality.

Parents who hurry need to be reminded of Ecker's Seventh Law: *It is impossible to control the events of life.* They also need to be reminded that, when a person demands such control, the results are universally destructive.

Parents can, however, control their own feelings. By undertaking a program of stress prevention, they can establish an identity that is founded on self-acceptance rather than on the developmental progress of their children. If they choose to do this, their children will be able to develop in an environment whose stability base is clearly rooted in parental love and sensitivity.

Parents nearly always understand that they are responsible for the health and safety of their children. Some find it harder to understand that it is also their responsibility to establish an environment that fosters emotional stability. In their own need for stress reduction, parents sometimes allow this latter responsibility to fall by the wayside. They substitute parental dominance—a tight control of their children's lives—for stability. When this happens, parent-child conflict is nearly inevitable—especially if the children are adolescents. This is because, as adolescents become increasingly capable of making adult judgments and perceptions, it is necessary for the parent-child relationship to change. It is no longer appropriate—and, in any case, it is practically impossible—for parents to continue to control every aspect of the lives of adolescent children.

Setting Limits
Parents guarantee stability for their children by establishing a family setting in which the unexpected is minimized and by defining limits to the children's activities outside that environment. Properly set and supervised, these limits restrict children's experiences to those with which they can deal at their current state of maturity. They insulate the children from circumstances that are likely to cause not only physical harm but also emotionally threatening instability.

They provide an element of certainty in the children's lives. Whatever happens beyond them, things are stable within the well-set limits.

In her book *The Hiding Place*, Corrie ten Boom tells an incident from her childhood which illustrates well the responsible setting of developmental limits. When, as a child of ten or eleven, Corrie asked her father to explain the term "sex sin," Mr. ten Boom responded by asking his daughter to carry his well-stuffed traveling case. She tried, but it was too heavy. Then her father explained that, like the traveling case, some knowledge is too heavy for children. For now, he explained, she would have to trust him to carry that burden for her. He had set some simple and effective limits for her—and she was left at peace in the assurance that she would not be required to confront an aspect of life for which she was not yet emotionally prepared.

For growing children, next to love, limits are the most important element of emotional stability the parents can provide. With limits, children always know that certain things in life are "for sure." Later, when they are older, they will be able to make their own perceptive judgments about what is and is not harmful and whether or not to react to uncertainty with stress. But we can't expect young children to make such adult judgments; so to protect them from personal harm and emotional instability, we insulate them from certain parts of the world. We set limits.

Imposed limits provide a temporary stability structure for children to use while they are developing their own identities. Young children are continuously collecting the guiding principles that they will use to give direction and purpose to their lives, but for some years their structure will be incomplete and unable to stand alone as their basis of emotional stability. Without limits, children can be expected to suffer frequent unnecessary stress during their development. The stability structure resulting from a stressful maturation process will be more insecure and less able to protect emotional stability in later life.

Parents need not apologize for establishing and enforcing limits, as long as these limits are set with the children's healthy development as their only purpose, and as long as they are imposed in accordance with the children's actual needs at the time. But problems arise when parents employ the setting of limits as a form of stress-motivated behavior—when they try to limit the child to control their own stress. Among relationships that involve sharing life control, the parent-child relationship is unique in one important aspect: society actually grants parents a tremendous amount of power to control the lives of their children. Thus it can be a great temptation for parents to try to avoid stress by using their authority to control their children's activities. But parents who do this always run into a major obstacle—adolescence.

As children mature, their experience increases and their ability to deal with the world expands. To permit normal developmental progress, children's limits need to be continually extended to keep pace with their expanding capabilities and insights. During the teen years, young people strive to assume personal responsibility for controlling their lives. This striving often conflicts with the attitudes and actions of a parent who is not prepared to let go, a parent who cannot give up control without experiencing stress. Typically, such parents play manipulative games to retain control, but such games nearly always make things worse.

Adolescents want—and have a right—to know why their parents have imposed limits on them. Limits based on the parents' realistic appraisal of the child's capabilities are not difficult to substantiate, even if not always to the adolescent's immediate satisfaction. But when parents can't honestly justify the limits they have set on the basis of the best interests of the child's development, then it is likely that these limits serve more to calm parental anxieties than to promote the child's healthy development.

Most adolescents are perceptive enough to know when they are being manipulated. They are aware of the game their parents are playing, even when the limits themselves are appropriate to the situation, if the motivation behind them is only to maintain parental control. Teen-agers are highly likely to reject unjustifiable limits as arbitrary and unfair and to use the situation as a basis for conflict. They can see their parents' confused attitude toward them, and they wonder why, if the parents are really concerned for them, they are less than honest about their motivations.

To illustrate, let's return briefly to the father we discussed earlier who had given his teen-aged daughter a midnight curfew. A curfew *is* a limit, a legitimate means of regulating a young person's developmental environment. Let us assume that, in this situation, the midnight curfew *was* a reasonable and valid limit. In that case, it *should have been* very possible for the parent to explain its validity to the child. But what if the father's only answer to his daughter's inevitable "Why?" is "Because I said so!"

Such a response clearly indicates to the child that the father's own anxiety, and not her welfare, is the primary basis for the limit he has set. Thus, as valid as the limit is, he has made it invalid in her view by imposing it as a mechanism to control his own stress rather than as a means of promoting her healthy emotional development.

The question is not whether parents should maintain authority over their adolescent children—clearly they should. The question is how this authority should be exercised. If it is exercised for the purpose of controlling parental stress, then the parents are abusing their power. The results will probably be a deterioration of the parent-child relationship and an increased likelihood of abnormal adolescent development. Limits should be imposed for the good of the child, not the convenience of the parent.

Testing Limits
It is important to look at stress from the adolescent's perspective.

Parents of adolescent children frequently report that the young
people seem to be constantly testing the limits, trying to find out
how far beyond them they can go before their parents clamp down
on them. Parents typically see this behavior as rebellion. They
consider it open defiance of parental authority, and they often use
a heavy hand to deal with it. But there is an alternate explanation
for the adolescent testing of parental limits, one that prompts a more
constructive response on the part of parents.

Adolescence is a time of rapid and extensive change, both in
children's physical and emotional make-up and in the way they see
the world. Change, of course, prompts a sense of instability; and
instability, in the life of someone who is not prepared to deal with
it, promotes unwanted stress. Indeed, adolescence is generally
considered one of the more stressful periods in life; the almost
epidemic problems of substance abuse and suicide among adolescents tend to substantiate this. But to what extent is stress the
natural consequence of an immature personality's emergence into
an increasingly complex world, and to what extent is it due to
inadequate nurturing by the family? I believe that the great majority
of adolescent stress is due to parents' failure to provide the support
necessary for normal, healthy development.

In a world in which almost nothing is certain, adolescents need
to know that their family members are "for sure"—they are there;
they care; they set limits; they are consistent. Just as a fortress wall
protects inhabitants from hostile attackers, appropriate limits
provide a haven of certainty for adolescents. If the limits are properly
set, young people can function with stability within their
boundaries, safely insulated by the family fortress against the
destabilizing influences beyond them. Then, as the children mature,
parents can expand their limits to include within their sphere of
control all the influences they are capable of managing.

For example, Mr. and Mrs. Stricter set limits that prohibit Ruth,
their fourteen-year-old, from serious dating. This makes it unneces-

sary for Ruth to try to sort through and understand the complexities of boy-girl relationships. Later, Ruth's parents lift this restriction when she is considered capable of understanding and dealing with mature relationships. But Mr. and Mrs. Stricter may still choose to exercise control—to set limits—over what movies she sees. They do not consider her capable yet of discriminating the moral issues presented in some films.

But if limits are so good for young people, if they provide such a welcomed sense of security, why do some adolescents seem to be continually testing them? Simply because they want to be reassured that the limits are there. They are checking to see what can be depended upon. Do their parents really care? Are they really firm in their resolve to protect their children from destabilizing influences in the world? How much of the world will they require the children to take on at this time? Teen-agers need to have these questions answered, so they push against the limits. If the limits have been set fairly with the young person's best interests in mind, and if they are found to be firm when tested, the young person will feel reassured rather than oppressed by their existence. After a few such tests, he is not likely to spend much more effort investigating the limits. He will have been assured of the things that matter most—life is secure and somebody cares.

If, on the other hand, an adolescent pushes against the limits and they give way, how will he react? With joy? No way! His primary basis of security is suddenly in jeopardy. What would you do if one day on your way to work you depressed the brake pedal the accustomed amount and nothing happened? Would you give up and say, "I guess I don't have any brakes"? Of course not. You would keep pushing on that brake pedal until you got a response—even if you had to push it all the way to the floor. Your survival would depend on it. Adolescents react no differently to mushy limits than you do to mushy brakes. In both cases, the motivation is survival.

What kind of message do adolescents get from limits that are inconsistent, tenuous or arbitrary? Intended or not, the message they read from their parents is "We don't care." Their one haven of stability is no longer guaranteed. And they will keep testing the limits, just as you would keep pumping the brakes, until they either find the true boundaries or conclude that they no longer exist. If they don't exist, it will confirm to them that their parents don't care and that they are on their own in a world for which they are, at best, only partially prepared.

There is, of course, another perfectly valid reason for adolescents to challenge parental limits. Just as hurrying can upset development by allowing limits too far beyond the child's adaptive capabilities, so parents can also impede the maturation process by making their limits too restrictive. And, as in the case of hurrying, such restrictions are typically stress motivated.

I pointed out earlier that one of the most difficult aspects of parenting is the need for continuously expanding developmental limits as the child matures. If the adjustment of limits does not keep pace with the child's increasing adaptability, parents can expect children to press on those limits as they strive to discover the full extent of their environment. Such limit testing is an expression of an unsatisfied need. Parents who attune themselves to these signals can learn a great deal about the emotional needs of their offspring— and about the effectiveness of their parenting.

Adolescents do not want to live without limits. Young people are content with any reasonable limits as long as they can read in the limits that somebody cares. The only adolescents who are likely to rebel against parental enforcement of limits are those who do not consistently receive limits that are firm and fair. I believe that the biggest problem parents experience in setting and enforcing reasonable limits for their adolescents is their own inability to deal honestly with their stress. Parenting adolescents is admittedly tough business. But if we first learn how to manage our own stress, we will be amazed at how much easier it is to manage our adolescents.

10 Stress and the Workplace

*A*RECENT MAGAZINE ARTICLE PRESENTED RESULTS FROM a survey of U.S. corporate leaders, documenting their viewpoints on stress in the workplace. According to these executives, their most frequent cause of stress was problems with personnel.

Any setting in which people are required to share some aspect of life control has the potential for generating stress. In the family, shared control results from the large emotional investment the members have made in one another. In the workplace, it more likely results from each worker's large investment in his or her own success. In the family, the investment is usually mutual: each member shares control with the others. In the workplace, by contrast, the investment frequently is not mutual. Worker X, for example, may be highly dependent on Worker Y for the completion of a task on which X's success depends. Worker Y, however, may have no significant investment either in the proper completion of the task or in Worker X's success.

The occurrence of stress in human relations does not depend on where the investment is made (at home or at work) or in whom (one's family or oneself). Rather, it depends on how much shared control that investment requires and on how willing an individual is to share that control. I share control whenever another person's activities can influence my emotional stability—that is, when events that are important to my stability are under the control of someone other than me. It is easy to see, then, why corporate executives so often attribute their stress to people problems. It is not hard to picture, for example, the extreme stress of a boss who has ambitious goals for success, but who is in charge of a work force that couldn't care less whether he reaches those goals.

It is important to remember that sharing control does not, of itself, cause stress. Stress occurs only when that dilution of personal control is perceived as a threat to stability, when life events are viewed as stressors. The main thing that makes stress in the workplace different from other kinds of stress is that its consequences are so easily measured in dollars and cents. We will approach the problem of work-related stress primarily from the perspective of the person to whom those dollars and cents are the most critical— the boss. We will look at his experience of stress, how that stress influences his employees' experience of stress and their job performance, and what he can do about it.

The Stress-Producing Boss

I once heard an employer describe his relationship with his work force this way: "I don't get ulcers—I give 'em!" Why does this man boast about his facility as an intimidator? Because that's the only way he knows to remain in control. He may or may not be immune to ulcers, but he certainly is not immune to stress. What he is really saying is this: "If they don't bow to my authority, I won't be in control. And if I'm not in control, I'll have stress."

Earlier I pointed out that there is no such thing as an intimidator—only people who allow themselves to be intimidated. This doesn't mean, however, that the boss has no responsibility for the way his or her employees respond. Of course each individual employee is responsible for his own stress, but if the employee does not handle his stress well and this stress affects his job performance, then the boss has a problem no matter who is responsible for the stress.

When Ms. Brittle bases her personnel-management style on her need to control her own stress, the workplace is an unpleasant environment and work performance suffers. The principle expressed in Ecker's Third Law—*Excess stress promotes excess stress*—is especially applicable in the work setting. An uptight Ms. Brittle is likely to have uptight and discontented employees. A stress-motivated management style often results in a low-key, workplace version of World War 3, with everyone more interested in his or her personal stability than in the goals of the business. No wonder Ms. Brittle would say her biggest source of stress is personnel problems.

Ms. Brittle's stress didn't originate with her employees. It originated with her unwillingness to share control over something of great importance to her—success in business. She needs the employees' help to accomplish that goal, so she has to share control with them. But she can't deal with not being in complete control herself. It causes uncertainty, threatens her stability and provokes stress. So to try to eliminate the stress, she manipulates her employees in an effort to regain control. In this classic example of stress-motivated behavior, it is the boss, not the work force, who is the main cause of stress.

The biggest single thing an employer or supervisor can do to help eliminate the problem of stress among employees is to get his own act together. Of course certain employees will always react to certain tasks with stress, and conflicts among individual employees can erupt even in the most congenial work settings. But such occurrences are not unique to the workplace; the people involved would probably provoke similar conflicts in any setting. The one aspect of work-related stress that is unique to the workplace is the supervisor's behavior toward employees. This is probably the most significant overall contributor to business-related stress.

Stress-motivated behavior can affect personnel administration at almost any level. If Mr. Withers allows his need for control to dominate his management style, it can have a major influence on the way he selects people, supervises them, rewards them and reacts to them himself. It can also significantly affect how the employees feel about themselves and how they respond to the boss and one another. Suppose Mr. Withers, out of his need for personal control, selects for a subordinate supervisory position Mr. Bumstead, a meek and cautious toady. In this selection, Mr. Withers has satisfied his need to remain personally in control. But what has he done to the workplace?

Mr. Bumstead is expected to do things the boss's way. But he was not selected for his abilities as a self-starter, and so he spends a great deal of time checking with Mr. Withers for support and direction. Is this situation satisfactory for the boss? Not at all. He may have selected Mr. Bumstead for his submissive qualities, but he still expects him to perform like a tiger—to be a carbon copy of the boss himself. In fact, Mr. Withers can't stand indecisiveness, berates Mr. Bumstead for his lack of initiative and continually gets involved in the supervisor's work. Meanwhile, Mr. Bumstead's work setting is in chaos from lack of supervision, oversupervision, conflicting instructions and just plain confusion.

On what does Mr. Withers blame this degenerative situation? You guessed it—personnel problems, caused mainly by the incompetent middle manager, Mr. Bumstead. It's a classic case of Ecker's Third Law at work in the workplace. Motivated by his own need to control, the boss makes an unwise personnel selection. This selection, however, does not provide him the hoped-for increase in control over events in the workplace. Instead, it actually decreases his control. In an effort to regain this lost control, the boss begins to manipulate the work setting. This increases uncertainty among the employees, elevates their experience of stress and diminishes their work performance. This further loss of control over important life events heightens the boss's already elevated stress level.

It is important for us to recognize that it is not specifically his selection of Mr. Bumstead as supervisor that is at the root of Mr. Withers's problem. The fundamental problem is his motivation for the selection—a motivation that is the basis of his whole approach to management—a driving need to control his own stress.

It really doesn't matter what kind of person Mr. Withers selects for the supervisor's job. Withers needs to be in complete control, and his willingness to manipulate anything and everything to assure that he stays in control guarantees that his workplace will always be a place of tension and conflict. Is this portrait of Mr. Withers exaggerated? Not at all. There is probably a bit of him in the majority of employers, and bosses who closely resemble him are abundant enough to have a name: they are called *controllers*. "Management by control"—controlling people for the primary purpose of avoiding stress—is prevalent enough in business environments that it is probably the primary cause of stress in the workplace.

Obviously all managers are required, as part of their job assignments, to be in charge of what takes place at work. They are expected to give directions and see that they are carried out. What is in question is the manager's need to maintain personal control as a mechanism for avoiding stress. Being in control is good management. Having to be in control invites disaster.

Capabilities, Expectations and Limits

It is important to understand three attributes of employer-employee relations in order to understand how management by control contributes to stress in the workplace. The first, *capabilities*, is the sum total of everything the employee brings to the work setting which can be used to perform his or her assigned task. The second, *expectations,* is the employer's standard of performance for the task. The employer then establishes the *limits* of a domain in which employee capabilities can be expressed and employer expectations can be realized. Of these three attributes, only capability is an established reality. Expectation and limits both relate to how that reality is dealt with by the employer.

Figure 8 presents a diagrammatic representation of these three attributes. The size of each square represents the magnitude of the attribute in relation to the other two. In the ideal management strategy, all three attributes should have the same magnitude. For maximum performance and employee satisfaction, the employee's capabilities should be equivalent to the employer's expectations, and the limits should allow the employee's capabilities to be fully expressed and the employer's expectations to be fully met. In ideal management strategy, the three squares coincide.

Employee Capabilities   Employer Expectations   Job Limits

Figure 8.   Three Attributes of Employer-Employee Relations

But what happens when, because of his need to control, the employer uses a management strategy that does not allow enough space for the employee's capabilities? Such management by control is a form of stress-motivated behavior on the part of the boss. The classic "controller," like Mr. Withers, uses both expectations and limits as tools in his stress-motivated manipulation.

First, he sets expectations that are beyond the employee's capabilities. The controller thinks there is only one right way to do the job—his way. His expectations are based more on how he sees himself performing the job than on how he might reasonably expect the employee to do it. The consequences are frustration and conflict all around. The employee struggles constantly against unreasonable demands, and the boss is perpetually frustrated by unmet expectations.

Then the controller further confuses the scenario by regulating— setting limits on—the employee's activities within the job. Job descriptions are unimportant to a controller. The only really important thing to him is control of the immediate situation and the hoped-for elimination of personal stress that this control represents for him. Therefore he will limit the employee's work activities to whatever extent needed to restore his own sense of control. Often he will end up doing the employee's task himself, all the while complaining about how hard it is to get good help these days. The employee, of course, is further confused, frustrated and demeaned by this action, which adds to his own burden of stress.

In management by control, the three boxes—employee's capabilities, employer's expectations, and limits—are not equal in size. Instead, they may look like figure 9. In this case, not only are the employer's expectations well beyond the employee's capabilities,

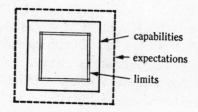

Figure 9.   The Results of Management by Control

but the boss has imposed such tight limits that the employee is not even permitted to work up to the capabilities he has.

Figure 9 shows just one of many management strategies in which capabilities, expectations and limits are out of balance with one another. However, employees will have a sense of stability—job satisfaction and freedom from stress-provoking pressures—only when the three attributes are in good balance and they are allowed to match their capabilities to their bosses' expectations and limits. When capabilities, expectations and limits are out of balance for any reason, employees can be expected to be less happy at work, less loyal to the company, less productive, more often the source of conflict, more likely to be absent or late, and more likely to quit or be terminated.

Employers, of course, end up being losers if they promote this kind of uncertainty in the on-the-job lives of their employees. Under such circumstances, they have to get the job done with a work force characterized by diminished incentive, increased conflict and high turnover. Yet some employers, notably the strong controllers, deal with such degenerating situations by continuing to try to manipulate their employees.

Perhaps the most fascinating of such manipulators are controllers who call themselves benevolent dictators. Mr. Kingman is one such employer who tries to buy submission to his controlling management style by giving his employees generous salaries and other incentives that don't cost him any immediate control over the events that are critical to his sense of stability. He feels that his benevolence earns him the right to dictate—to control absolutely everything. However, like all manipulations, this one has little chance of either relieving Mr. Kingman's stress or calming the anxiety and conflict within his work setting.

Whatever the source of stress in the workplace and whatever its immediate and long-range consequences in terms of productivity, it is clear that the boss is in charge of the solution. If things are going to change in the work setting, the boss will have to be personally behind that change. As Harry S Truman said, "The buck stops here." This is not to say that employees would not benefit from instruction in personal stress prevention. It merely acknowledges that high levels of stress don't happen in a work setting without a significant contribution from the person in charge.

Just as the stress that occurs in the workplace is qualitatively no different from the stress that occurs in other settings, so the process needed to prevent that stress is the same as for stress prevention in general. All of Ecker's Laws apply to the understanding and prevention of stress at work. The only way to succeed in the stress-prevention process is to go through the six steps described in chapters five and six, accepting reality for what it is, accepting responsibility when appropriate and accepting personal change as the cost of making it happen.

11 The Importance of Stress Prevention

*W*E HAVE NOW LOOKED AT WHAT STRESS IS, WHAT ITS consequences can be in various situations and how we can keep it from occurring. We know that stress is a physical reaction that occurs in the human body in response to a perceived threat to its stability and that it is intended only to serve the body's immediate physical requirements. When a stress response goes beyond those requirements, the excess stress promotes a variety of undesirable consequences. Managing stress, then, becomes a matter of understanding and controlling stress responses by correctly interpreting events and situations. Stress analysis helps us understand our own stress and react appropriately to stress-motivated behavior in others.

A New View
The ultimate step in the process of stress prevention is changing the

way we view ourselves and our place in the world. If I can make these changes, I can be freed from my captivity to unwanted stress. No longer will I hold onto my lifelong belief that events in the world around me threaten my personal identity. I will understand that my identity in the image of God is secure and that my life has special value quite apart from environmental influences. I can be certain of who I am, no matter what happens in the world around me.

Unwanted stress permeates virtually every aspect of modern American life. It can undermine human relationships and lead to conflict, unhappiness and abnormal emotional development. The dynamics of stress production are the same in any setting—at school, in government bodies, in the military, as well as at home and at work. Stress reactions are no different whether the participants are world leaders at a summit conference or second graders in a sandbox. Whatever their positions or circumstances, people react with unwanted stress for one reason—they are unable or unwilling to deal honestly with reality. It is not difficult to observe stress reactions in other people. If we take the time to look for the motivations behind stress-motivated behavior patterns, we will find it easier to identify and deal with such behavior in ourselves.

Stress, in my opinion, is the most significant negative factor at work in modern society. In fact, because its consequences can extend so far beyond the stressed individual, I believe that stress is the prime force behind virtually all destructive human behavior. Medically, one person's stress can affect only one person. Socially, on the other hand, it can affect many people.

Alcoholism, for example, is a predominantly stress-motivated disease that affects the health of no one but the alcoholic. If, however, the problem drinker has a family of six and supervises another ten people at work, the lives of at least sixteen people can be significantly influenced by this unfortunate choice of how to react to life.

Most violence is also stress motivated. One has only to look through the daily paper to see how one individual's violent acts can influence the lives of large segments of society. A murderer affects not only his victim and the victim's family and friends; he also affects everyone who hears about his crime and reacts with fear or anger.

In fact, almost all of the common social problems confronting our society have their roots in the stress reactions of the people involved. Street crime and drug abuse, for example, are the actions of people trying to deal with life's uncertainties. We try to prevent crime by enlarging our police forces, building bigger prisons and imposing stiffer sentences. We try to curb drug abuse by stopping the drug traffic. And yet both crime and drug abuse continue to increase. If these and other major social problems occur because people are unable to deal constructively with their stress, and if stress can be prevented, then it would make sense for us to deal with these problems at their common origin—the stress reactions of the people involved. If society is suffering because some of its members find themselves severely threatened by uncertainty, then the obvious solution is to help these people learn how to deal with their uncertainties.

Certainty in an Uncertain World
The events of life will never be certain for anyone. Yet uncertainty does not have to dominate anyone's life—because the really important things are certain for everyone. The author of the letter to the Hebrews said it best: "Jesus Christ is the same yesterday and today and for ever" (Heb 13:8). When our lives are founded on trust in the redeeming work of Jesus Christ, there is no uncertainty that matters.

I hope that in this book I have helped make this truth a reality for you. I hope I have helped you understand the extreme importance of stress prevention not only in your own life and health, but also in the life and health of society as a whole. And I hope I have given you some incentives and guidelines for making stress prevention a part of your life. Our life and our health will be immeasurably enriched if we make the elimination of unwanted stress a primary goal in life.

Appendix A
Ecker's Laws

1. If the stress is unwanted and unpleasant, it is always excessive to the physical needs of the circumstances.

2. If the stress response is greater than the need, the perception is always wrong.

3. Excess stress promotes excess stress.

4. Power to control feelings is never taken; it is only given away.

5. When you give away power, the other person never becomes more powerful—but you always become more powerless.

6. Stress prevention is carried out in the first person singular.

7. It is impossible to control the events of life.

8. If you have a problem with unwanted stress, you have a problem with your self-concept.

9. The price of stress prevention is personal change.

10. The greater your problem with stress, the more unwilling you will be to admit your need for change and the more difficulty you will have implementing the change.

11. Stress will not alter the outcome.

12. You don't need stress to care.

Appendix B
The Stress-Prevention Process

I Can
Step 1—Understand what stress is.
Step 2—Accept the responsibility for my own stress.
Step 3—Find out the real identity of the source.
Step 4—Get in touch with my own identity.

I Want To
Step 5—Count the cost.

I Will
Step 6—Commit to change.

Appendix C
Drugs and Stress

Much of the stress we experience is induced through the action of certain adrenal hormones. Normally, these hormones are released in the body in direct response to some external stress-provoking stimulus. But, stress can also be produced by certain drugs—drugs which promote the activity of these hormones in the body or directly mimic their stress-inducing action. These drug-induced stress reactions must be classed as an adaptive response because once the drug has been consumed, the stress response is inevitable. In this case, the stress is not a matter of conscious choice—it is a matter of metabolic necessity. The only way to reduce or avoid this kind of stress is to reduce or avoid the use of the drug.

Although the most powerful of the stress-inducing drugs are classified as controlled substances and can only be obtained legally by prescription, the most frequently used of the stress-provoking drugs are readily available without prescription. The prescription drugs, represented by the amphetamines, can cause severe stress reactions and can, when abused, promote habitual use. Cocaine, a currently popular street drug, is also classified generally as a stimulant (stress inducer). However, these controlled drugs are of little significance to average individuals who may be concerned about their major sources of stress. The naturally occurring and nonprescription stimulants, on the other hand, are very significant potential sources of stress for the average individual.

The most popular stress-producing drugs in use today can be divided into three general groups. The first of these groups contains several close, but nonprescription, relatives of amphetamine. These substances are frequently used as decongestants and nonprescription diet aids. The most commonly used of these are phenylpropanolamine and pseudoephedrine. These compounds, like their more powerful relative amphetamine, are chemically very similar to adrenalin and tend to mimic or stimulate its effects in the body. As we learned earlier, adrenalin is one of the body's prime mediators of the stress response.

Figure 10, although by no means an exhaustive list, shows some popular, nonprescription sources of phenylpropanolamine and pseudoephedrine. Some of the products also contain caffeine, which will be discussed later.

Note that the cold formulas listed in figure 10 generally allow much more of the primary stress-provoking drug per day than do the appetite suppressants. This is particularly fascinating when you consider that most of the diet drugs declare on the label that the dosage recommended is the maximum allowable for that use. For example, Dietac (an anarexic) and Formula 12 (a decongestant) are identical in formulation. Yet the decongestant permits twice the daily intake of the same drug. This is not to suggest that you should interchange uses of these drugs; only that you should read the labels carefully to understand clearly what you are getting and in what amounts. And, if you remain unconvinced that these drugs can produce stress, just check the labels for the symptoms they recommend as reasons for discontinuing use of the drug. They are all stress reactions as I have described them here.

The second group of stress drugs consists of caffeine and several of its related compounds. These drugs occur naturally in coffee, tea and cocoa, and are added to cola drinks and a number of drug formulations, particularly certain pain remedies and so-called stay-alert pills. Caffeine is also used in combination with phenylpropanolamine in some diet drugs. Like the amphetamine derivatives just discussed, caffeine and its close relatives mimic or promote a number of activities of adrenalin.

Most of the caffeine consumed in the United States comes from two natural products: coffee and tea. In fact, Americans now consume an average of over one-third of a pound of caffeine per person per year from these two sources alone. Cocoa contains a close chemical relative of caffeine. Figure 11 shows the amount of caffeine contributed by various forms of these natural products, by soft drinks to which caffeine has been added and by several representative nonprescription pharmaceutical preparations which contain the drug. Caffeine amounts in drug products which also contain phenylpropanolamine were listed in figure 10. In compiling these lists, I do not in any way suggest that you should necessarily avoid these products or similar products which were not listed. It is my purpose only to make you aware of the presence and the quantities of stress-provoking drugs in these kinds of products. Any specific questions about their use should be referred to your physician.

The third group of stress-inducing substances are those which contain nicotine. Available mostly from tobacco products (particularly cigarettes), nicotine stimulates the activity of stress hormones in the body. This causes several typical stress reactions, including an increase in heart rate and blood pressure and the constriction of certain blood vessels. The amount of nicotine

	Drug	Content Per Dose	Maximum Recommended Doses Per Day	Total Dosage Allowed Per Day	Other Ingredients
Anorexics = Diet Drugs					
Dexatrim	PPA CAF	50 Mg 200 Mg	1	50 Mg 200 Mg	None
Extra- Strength Dexatrim	PPA CAF	75 Mg 200 Mg	1	75 Mg 200 Mg	None
Appedrine	PPA CAF	25 Mg 100 Mg	3	75 Mg 300 Mg	10 Vitamins
Dietac	PPA	75 Mg	1	75 Mg	None
Cold Formulas					
Sudafed	PE	30 Mg	8	240 Mg	None
Sudafed Plus	PE	60 Mg	4	240 Mg	AH
Dristan Caps.	PPA CAF	12.5 Mg 16.2 Mg	6	75 Mg 97 Mg	ASP, AH
Contac	PPA	75 Mg	2	150 Mg	AH
Sinutab	PPA	25 Mg	6	150 Mg	AH, AAP
Allerest	PPA	18.7 Mg	8	150 Mg	AH, AAP
Formula 12	PPA	75 Mg	2	150 Mg	None

PPA = Phenylpropanolamine   AH = Antihistamine
PE = Pseudoephedrine   ASP = Aspirin
CAF = Caffeine   AAP = Acetaminophen (non-aspirin pain reliever)

Information in figures 10 and 11 on ingredient contents and dosages of commercial products were obtained from the product labels. Information on caffeine content in natural products was obtained from B. A. Kihlman, *Caffeine and Chromosomes* (Amsterdam: Elsivier, 1977), pp. 11-51.

Figure 10. Stress-Producing Drugs: Amphetamine Relatives

Trade or Common Name	Dose or Serving Size	Caffeine Content Per Dose or Serving	Recommended Maximum Doses Per Day	Maximum Caffeine Intake Per Day	Other Ingredients
Natural Products					
Coffee	1 Cup	75-135 Mg	—	—	—
Tea	1 Cup	75-110 Mg	—	—	—
Hot Chocolate*	1 Cup	75-150 Mg	—	—	—
Bittersweet Chocolate*	1 Oz.	150-300 Mg	—	—	—
Milk Chocolate*	1 Oz.	75-150 Mg	—	—	—
Soft Drinks					
Colas	12 Fl. Oz.	20-55 Mg	—	—	—
Analgesics = Pain Relievers					
Anacin	Each	32 Mg	10	320 Mg	ASP
Excedrin	Each	65 Mg	8	550 Mg	ASP, AAP
Vanquish	Each	33 Mg	12	396 Mg	ASP, AAP, BUF
Cope	Each	32 Mg	8	256 Mg	ASP, BUF
Stimulants					
No Doz	Each	100 Mg	9	900 Mg	None
Vivarin	Each	200 Mg	6	1200 Mg	None

*The primary stimulant in cocoa is not caffeine but a closely related compound with a similar effect on the body.

ASP = Aspirin
AAP = Acetaminophen (non-aspirin pain reliever)
BUF = Buffer

Figure 11. Stress-Producing Drugs: Caffeine

consumed per cigarette varies widely from brand to brand, but the stress response to the drug is measurable in almost all cases. In fact, some authorities feel that this particular drug effect is the primary factor in the contribution of smoking to the occurrence of heart disease.

Stress is a difficult reaction to measure in exact terms. So there is no specific information available on the relationship between drug dose and the amount of stress produced. We do know that the drugs which we have identified as "stress-inducing" cause changes in those physical responses we have identified with stress; such reactions as heart rate and blood pressure. But the best we can do in relating the intake of the drug to the occurrence of stress is to say that, in the doses commonly used, the stress response is measurable and that the amount of stress experienced increases with the dose. The specific experience of stress can also be expected to vary from individual to individual and from drug to drug.

Whatever your specific reaction to stress-inducing drugs, you should be aware that any stress you experience from this source contributes some amount to your total daily stress burden and that this stress will be unnecessary and, thus, inappropriate to your need. This amount may be insignificant in your life, or it may be a major contributor to your personal stress. If you are looking for ways to decrease your total experience of stress, a change in your use of these drugs may provide a simple and significant beginning.

Appendix D
Diet and Stress

Several years ago a scientific study published by the American Chemical Society revealed some rather startling information on the role of diet in the human stress response. This study showed that the average American on a typical American diet can expect about one-third of all his or her stress to be caused by the diet. (See J. D. Palm, *Diet Away Your Stress, Tension and Anxiety* [Garden City, N.Y.: Doubleday & Co., 1976].) In some people, the proportion may be greater than two-thirds. This very large potential influence of diet on the stress response makes it essential that we consider how stress can be caused by what we eat, and how diets can be designed to minimize this source of stress.

To do so, we first need to know something about how the body regulates the availability of fuel for the brain. The brain uses energy continuously and has a constant need for a large amount of fuel. In addition, among the several fuel sources generally available in the body, the brain can normally use only one, and this is the one that is the least plentiful. As a result, the brain is engaged in a continual effort to assure an adequate supply of fuel. Under all conditions except long-term fasting, the brain can use only blood sugar as a fuel. On the average, the total amount of this fuel available in the body at any time is about 5 grams, or the equivalent of about one level teaspoon of sugar. However, the brain uses up about 3½ grams of blood sugar in just one hour in order to satisfy its regular energy requirements. So, the body has to use some very special mechanisms to keep up the supply of this very critical fuel.

Sugars, as a group, are the basic units which make up the class of foods we call carbohydrates. Sugars, in their simple form, are found in foods such as fruits and sweets. They also occur in a more complex form called starch, which is found in grains, potatoes and other starchy vegetables. Starch is made up of long chains of individual sugar units. When carbohydrate foods are digested in the body, these simple sugar units are released in the intestine and are picked up in the blood stream, where they become blood sugar.

The digestive system, however, has no control over how much sugar is produced from its digestion of carbohydrate foods. It digests all of the carbohydrate it is supplied and converts this carbohydrate into blood sugar. So, if a meal contains a large amount of carbohydrate, and this carbohydrate is rapidly digested, a large amount of blood sugar can be produced in a very short time. This, in turn, can cause a rapid increase in the level of sugar in the blood. However, in keeping with its tendency to maintain stability in all things, the body reacts against any substantial change in its internal environment. So, in the normal individual, a rapid increase in blood sugar level is dealt with immediately and decisively. To accomplish this, the body uses the hormone insulin.

Insulin regulates the disposal of excess blood sugar and directs how it will be used in the body. Some of the sugar will be stored away in the liver as a blood sugar reserve, for use later when the supply of sugar in the blood begins to run low. Some of it will be stored in the muscles for use as a fuel for muscular contraction. Some of it will be made into fat. In general, the more rapidly the blood sugar increases from the digestion of carbohydrate foods in the diet, the larger the insulin response that the body will produce in reaction to the change. And, the greater the insulin response, the less the amount of blood sugar that will be stored in the liver and muscles, and the more that will be converted into fat.

During the times between meals, when blood sugar is not being supplied by the digestion of food, the continual need for blood sugar by the body (an average 3½ grams per hour for the brain alone) will tend to use up the limited supply of this fuel, and the blood sugar level will begin to decrease. When this happens, the body will again react to preserve its internal stability. In this case, the regulating mechanism is *stress*.

This stress response causes the release of sugar previously stored in the liver and causes additional sugar to be manufactured from other substances in the body, primarily protein. The result is an increase in blood sugar level and a return of the body's chemical environment to a state of stability. But, for a period of time, the body will have been under some amount of stress. I classify this kind of stress response as adaptive because, once the shortage of fuel (blood sugar) has occurred, the stress response will happen automatically as a nonconscious, physiological reaction. But, it is important to recognize that, like the stress produced from the use of drugs, dietary stress causes the same effects on the body as does stress from any more obvious source. The source may be different—but the stress is the same.

A more difficult question is, How much of this stress might be excessive to the body's physical need and, thus, would be experienced as unpleasant and unwanted? There is no doubt that the stress which is involved in blood sugar control can and does cause noticeable, undesirable stress. This fact is easily verified by any of us who have experienced midmorning or midafternoon episodes of such classic stress symptoms as headache, nervousness, tension, irritability and reduced ability to concentrate. Yet, because this kind of stress insures survival in a different way than the typical "fight or flight" reaction, we don't really know how much stress is needed to cause proper blood sugar control and how much, if any, of the actual response might be excessive to that need. From clinical research, we do know that certain dietary excesses do cause increases in total daily stress and that much of this stress can be eliminated by altering the diet. It could be, therefore, that only a certain minimum amount of stress is required to insure correct blood sugar control and that the greater amounts caused by dietary excesses are experienced as excess stress.

We also know, however, that symptoms of excess stress can be experienced by some people who simply delay too long between meals. This stress is not a reaction to the diet but is a simple response to a slowly depleting fuel supply. Thus, it may be that *all* of the stress involved in blood sugar control is excess stress as we have defined it (that is, greater than that needed by the body to deal physically with a threat to its stability), and that the experience of this excess is simply one of the things that happens in the early stages of brain fuel starvation.

This theory, which I call functional overlap, is the one I favor personally. An increase in blood sugar, which is required to assure fuel for the brain, is one of the normal reactions in the "fight or flight" response. I suggest that, if an increase in blood sugar is needed at times when no physical threat exists, the only mechanism available in the body to fulfill this need is stress. Since none of the other "fight or flight" reactions is needed in this situation, the stress which is produced to control blood sugar is excess stress in every other respect, and is experienced as such. When the diet and individual responsiveness are normal, this excess stress experience will be minimal. But when the diet is abusive to the control system and/or when an individual has a fundamental problem with blood sugar control, this diet-induced experience of excess stress can be substantial.

With this understanding of the mechanisms by which the body controls the availability of fuel for the brain (blood sugar), it should be clear that dietary stress will be prevented to whatever extent it is possible to maintain blood sugar above the stress-inducing level. To learn how this is possible, we need to know something more about the major causes of temporary low blood sugar, or hypoglycemia.

The normally limited amount of blood sugar in the body is being used up constantly at a high rate to fulfill the energy requirements of the brain and other tissues. Thus, a blood sugar supply that is not supplemented from the diet will soon fall to a level which will require a stress response for correction. However, the diet itself can often be a major cause of stress-inducing low blood sugar. This is because of the action of insulin. As we discussed earlier, increases in blood sugar above the normal range cause the body to produce insulin, which serves to keep the level from going too high and assists the body in disposing of the sugar. This action of insulin causes a decrease in the blood sugar level. But, a problem can occur if this blood sugar decrease becomes so great that the level goes below normal and requires a stress response to get it back to normal. We can call this occurrence reactive hypoglycemia. Such reactive responses occur most often following very rapid increases in the blood sugar level.

To assure a stable blood sugar level and to avoid frequent episodes of hypoglycemic stress, eating patterns should be adjusted to avoid rapid increases in blood sugar. The diet should be designed to permit slow and steady increases in blood sugar following digestion. This will have the effect of continuously resupplying blood sugar between meals, as the fuel is being used up in the body for the production of energy. Such stability in blood sugar level will minimize the need for corrective stress responses. We can, in fact, substantially decrease our stress simply by changing the way we eat.

In general, the simpler the form of the carbohydrate in a food, the more easily it will be digested and converted into blood sugar. Thus, the simple sugars themselves produce the most rapid increases in blood sugar and are the most likely to cause reactive stress responses, especially if they are consumed in large amounts. On the other hand, if the carbohydrate foods contain mostly starch, and if that starch is itself combined into a complex structure within the food, then the digestion of the carbohydrate will be delayed and blood sugar will be produced more slowly. This will minimize the possibility of a significant insulin response and will allow the digestive system to supply blood sugar at a rate more equivalent to its need by the body. The result will be a more stable blood sugar level and a reduction in the body's need for stabilizing stress responses.

Figure 12 illustrates the difference between the kind of blood sugar response that is produced by simple sugars and that produced by complex carbohydrate foods. In this figure, Curve 1 shows a typical blood sugar response to a 12-ounce serving of a regular, sugar-sweetened soft drink. In less than two hours, the blood sugar is lower than it was at the outset and on its way to a level that will require a stress response for recovery. Curve 2 shows the expected blood sugar response from a serving of coarse-ground whole-wheat bread that contains the same amount of carbohydrate as that in the soft drink. (Soft drinks contain about 35 grams—7 teaspoons—of sugar; roughly the same amount of carbohydrate as you would obtain in 3 slices of bread.) In normal people, complex carbohydrate foods produce a slower blood sugar increase and they sustain a desirable blood sugar level for several hours. During this time, no stress is required to assure the body's supply of brain fuel.

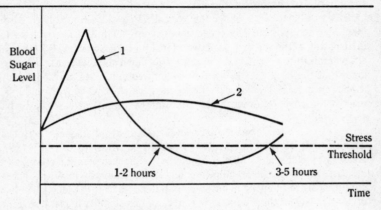

Curve 1: Response to sugar-sweetened soft drink.
Curve 2: Response to whole wheat bread.

Figure 12. Two Typical Blood Sugar Responses

There is one notable exception to the observation that simple sugars produce rapid increases in blood sugar. This exception is the sugar fructose, or fruit sugar. Unlike other simple sugars, fructose is only slowly absorbed into the blood and causes no release of insulin. Thus, the body's response to the intake of fructose is more like Curve 2 above, and stress responses have been shown to decrease when fructose is the primary carbohydrate used in the diet.

The blood sugar reactions that result from large insulin responses, such as that in Curve 1, have the added disadvantage that the high insulin levels tend to convert much of the excess blood sugar into fat. This means that a smaller amount of the carbohydrate consumed will be available for storage in the liver as a blood sugar reservoir. Thus, if much of the carbohydrate consumed during the day results in Curve 1 reactions, not only will reactive stress responses be frequent, they will tend to last for longer periods because of the shortage of sugar reserves in the liver.

Clearly, if we hope to minimize dietary stress, our consumption of carbohydrates should produce, as much as possible, responses like Curve 2. The following guidelines should be helpful in accomplishing this goal:

1. Minimize your intake of foods containing large amounts of easily digested simple sugars—foods such as sugar-sweetened soft drinks, candy,

desserts and pastries.

2. When simple sugars are consumed, limit the amount taken at any one time or, preferably, use fructose as a substitute sweetener.

3. Emphasize foods in the diet which provide the more complex, slowly digested, sources of carbohydrate—such foods as whole-grain cereals and breads, brown rice, corn and raw or lightly cooked vegetables.

4. Eat smaller meals of more equal size and replace the calories with substantial snacks two or three times per day, so that significant blood sugar increases will be minimized.

5. Never skip meals.

Diet-induced stress is preventable; not by controlling the stress response, but by controlling the event that provokes the need for stress—the starvation of the brain for fuel. A small amount of attention to this one fundamental factor could well eliminate a significant amount of your unwanted stress.